DANGERS
TOILS & SNARES

Mastering Ministry's Pressure Points

DANGERS
TOILS & SNARES

Resisting the Hidden Temptations of Ministry

RICHARD EXLEY
MARK GALLI
JOHN ORTBERG

MULTNOMAH BOOKS

Contents

Part 3
The Long View

Introduction

The Wednesday after the Sunday he preached on handling lust, Pastor Russ received a phone call from his best friend's wife. She and her husband had befriended Russ and his wife when they arrived to pastor the church. Their families had even vacationed together.

"Sunday you preached on sexual obsessions," she began, "and I need to confess an obsession I have."

Russ stiffened. *Do I want to hear about this from a friend?* he thought.

"Frankly, my obsession has to do with you," she said. "I've

been waiting some time to tell you that I'm in love with you."

Russ drew a long breath. His mouth felt parched, his heart quickened.

What now? he thought wildly. Part of him wanted to listen; he was flattered that Barb had found him attractive. Part of him panicked: *I've got to stop this pronto. I can't listen to this.*

"Stop right there," Russ said firmly. "I don't want to hear it."

"But I have these feelings for you that won't go away. I just want to come and . . ."

"Stop it, Barb," he said, raising his voice.

"Can't we just talk about it? Maybe it will help."

"No, we can't talk about it. And if you continue, I'll have to hang up the phone."

"But I have to talk about it, and I have to talk with you . . ."

"Barb, I'm hanging up the phone. I'm sorry. Good-bye."

Russ's response — refusing to hear her passion for him — effectively crushed sin's call before it became alluring. Temptation never got an audience. That's because, at least in this area, Russ was spiritually fit.

Fighting sin is akin to staying physically fit. As my chest and stomach have begun to sag due to age and benign neglect, I've learned a principle about weight control: it's easier to control fat than reduce it.

This principle assumes I'll always longingly eye that fourth and fifth piece of pepperoni and mushroom pizza. My appetite will always outstrip my metabolism. Temptation will be a constant companion. But it's a lot easier to battle the temptation to overeat when at 160 pounds than 175, when I'm already fit rather than all too fat.

Russ resisted temptation at its onset, demonstrating a spiritual fitness we would all like to have.

The three authors of the fifth Mastering Ministry's Pressure Points book have felt the pressure of ministry's darker side. Like Russ — like all of us — they've battled lust, ambition, discouragement, and cowardice, to name a few of the subtle and not-so-subtle temptations of ministry. These leaders offer stories of triumph and tragedy, and they offer principles to help us get and stay spiritually fit.

John Ortberg

John Ortberg's professional training in psychology often gives him insight into his own quirks.

He writes, "The discipline of service probably comes least naturally for me. One of the chief places I've tried to practice this discipline is at home. I'm often tempted to play *I've Had a Harder Day than You, and I Deserve to Be Taken Care of by You* with my wife. (Being a pastor is worth bonus points in this game. I'm not only doing work, I'm doing God's work.)"

It's this refreshing honesty that helps John cut to the heart of any issue. In writing on the spiritual disciplines, he says, "Has practicing the disciplines made me a better pastor? I don't know. I hesitate to ask; one of my problems is the tendency to measure everything in terms of career enhancement. . . . The main thing I've gotten from the disciplines so far is hope — that the effort to become more like Christ has a definite shape. It's no longer just a vague desire. There are things I can do. And, given a lifetime, real change is possible."

John earned an M.Div. and a Ph.D. in psychology from Fuller Theological Seminary in Pasadena, California. He pastored Simi Valley Community Church in Simi Valley, California, for four years and presently is senior pastor of Horizons Community Church in Diamond Bar, California. He is also a frequent contributor to LEADERSHIP magazine.

Richard Exley

Richard Exley cares about pastors. Even before the subject became the rage, he had already written a book helping pastors to avoid sexual immorality (*The Perils of Power*).

In that book and in his ministry with pastors and spouses wounded by immorality, he has balanced high biblical moral standards with a compassionate touch. He writes, "Following the release of my book, *Perils of Power*, I began receiving calls and visits from fallen ministers and their spouses. Although their circumstances differed, they all shared at least one thing in common — devastation.

"In every case, I found myself face to face with immorality's tragic consequences. A pastor ensnared by adultery, or some other moral failure, usually loses his position, his income, and often his residence. Not infrequently, he is forced to leave the very community that should be giving him emotional support. He will be asked to confess publicly and resign all hard-won places of honor.

"No longer can he pretend to be a godly man of spiritual and moral integrity. Now everyone knows, now everywhere he turns his shameful failure confronts him. His confession has destroyed the faith placed in him by his peers, his trusting congregation, his family."

Richard's concern and wisdom comes from twenty-six years in pastoral ministry. Ten of those years he spent at Christian Chapel (Assemblies of God) in Tulsa, Oklahoma, which, under his leadership, grew from 100 to over 1,000 attenders. He is also a prolific author, having written, among others, *The Perils of Power*, *Blue Collar Christianity*, and *The Rhythm of Life*.

Currently a free-lance writer and minister-at-large working out of Tulsa, Richard produces a daily radio feature called "Straight from the Heart."

Mark Galli

Mark Galli is a colleague of mine at Christianity Today, Inc. In the two years I've known him, I've learned a principle about our relationship: You can take Mark flyfishing, but you can't teach him how to flyfish.

Mark recently picked up flyfishing with the same intensity he has for preaching and writing. On a recent business trip to Colorado, I attempted to coach him in the art of fly casting: putting an imitation bug, no bigger than the head of a pencil, onto the surface of a still and glassy high-mountain lake — without scaring the trout away. It was not easy.

"Uh, why don't you shorten your cast," I gingerly advised after an hour of fishing. "You'll have much more control."

By this time, I had caught five cutthroat trout to Mark's none. I could sense Mark's growing frustration, and I could see his problem. He was trying to cast too far out into the lake. With no control over his line, he was slapping it wildly onto the calm surface of the lake, beating the water to a froth. The trout, I'm sure, were chuckling from the far side of the lake.

"If I cast any closer to shore," Mark snapped, "I'll be wasting my time." Mark continued in his errant way.

A while later, he challenged another bit of flyfishing acumen. When we had purchased our tackle from a sporting shop in Aspen, the shopkeeper, an expert in flyfishing, advised us to buy a smaller-size fly: "In mountain lakes, you don't catch any fish with large flies. The smaller the better." I knew this to be true from my own experience.

Now Mark had pulled out a fly at least twice as big as this expert recommended. I snorted inwardly but kept my thoughts to myself.

The next thing I knew, Mark was reeling in what turned out to be the biggest trout of the day: a 14-inch, deep-girthed cutthroat.

When it comes to Christian life and ministry, Mark often chafes at the standard assumptions most of us operate by. That, as he readily admits, is not always wise; in most instances, standard assumptions are standard for good reason: they help people live effectively for Christ. Then again, because of his contrariness, Mark sometimes makes the biggest catch: he comes up with keen and fresh insights into the life of the Spirit.

Mark served as a Presbyterian pastor for ten years, in churches in Mexico City and Sacramento, California. He is associate editor of CHRISTIAN HISTORY magazine, host of the PREACHING TODAY cassette series, and contributing editor to LEADERSHIP. He is also co-author of the forthcoming book, *Preaching That Connects* (Zondervan).

Nowhere in Scripture is the Christian leader promised a

sabbatical from the wiles of the devil. Not even while doing God's work. We are, though, promised victory if we resist Satan's advances. We hope this book can contribute to victory.

— *David Goetz*
assistant editor, LEADERSHIP

Part 1
Dangers of Pastoral Toil

Most of the time, we fall short of holiness because we strive so diligently for holiness.

— Mark Galli

The Perils of Professional Holiness

Pick a century, any century, and you'll find lots of good advice given to pastors. In the sixth century, for instance, Pope Gregory, "the Great," wrote a whole book for pastors called *Pastoral Care*. In the middle of that book, he outlined the ideal pastoral lifestyle, or what some might call pulpit-committee utopia.

The pastor, he wrote, "must devote himself entirely to setting an ideal of living. He must die to all passions of the flesh and . . . lead a spiritual life."

All well and good if you stick to generalities. Gregory doesn't.

"He must have put aside worldly prosperity; he must fear no adversity, desire only what is interior. . . . He is not led to covet the goods of others, but is bounteous in giving of his own."

Certainly. Well, most of the time anyway.

"He is quickly moved by a compassionate heart to forgive, yet never so diverted from perfect rectitude as to forgive beyond what is proper."

Let's just say pastors manage this delicate balance every so often.

"He does no unlawful act himself while deploring those of others, as if they were his own. In the affection of his own heart he sympathizes with the frailties of others, and so rejoices in the good done by his neighbor, as though the progress made were his own."

No tasty resentment of spiteful elders? No gossip or jealousy of Pastor Homogeneous at Mega-Growth Community Church?

"In all that he does, he sets an example so inspiring to all others, that in their regard he has no cause to be ashamed of his past. He so studies to live as to be able to water the dry hearts of others with the streams of instruction imparted."

Yeah, and the Pope is Protestant.

Yet Gregory is right. This is precisely what it means to be a pastor or Christian leader, because this is what it means to be a Christian. It's only reasonable to expect teachers of Christian virtues and leaders of Christian congregations first to model Christian behaviors.

The call to pastoral holiness, then, is right. It's reasonable. It's also ridiculous.

Not because Christian leaders are slothful, though sometimes we are. Not because we don't care, though sometimes we don't. No, most of the time, we fall short of holiness because we strive so diligently for holiness.

Bonaventure, the great Franciscan leader, put it this way: "The devil is most eager to worm his way in where he recognizes that people are trying to live virtuously; he wants to seek out the innocent man and destroy him just where he was hoping to give himself to God's service."

This is especially true of those involved in "full-time Christian service." In his book *The Unpredictable Plant*, Eugene Peterson writes, "The moment any of us embarks on work that deals with our fellow humans at the core and depths of being where God and sin and holiness are at issue, we become at that same moment subject to countless dangers, interferences, pretenses, and errors that we would have been quite safe from otherwise. So-called 'spiritual work' exposes us to spiritual sins."

Spiritual Sins

Christian leaders usually fret about the sins that stroll down the center of Soul Boulevard:

"I need to forgive the chairman for those remarks."

"If I were more disciplined during the week, I wouldn't have to come in on my day off."

"Can't I counsel an attractive woman without fantasizing about her?"

Fleshly sins — anger, sloth, lust — are at least obvious. No mistaking what's going on here. These are SINS.

Spiritual sins, though, come disguised as virtues, virtues Christian leaders, as men and women of God, long to attain. But they are sins nonetheless. I'm talking about hypocrisy and pride.

Take hypocrisy, which comes in a variety of forms.

In some cases, for instance, we start calling evil *good*. When it comes to holy living, our desire far outstrips our practice, so we sometimes manage that frustration by naming our terms.

Gregory the Great said that with pastors "vices commonly masquerade as virtues. Often, for instance, a niggard passes himself off as frugal, while one who is prodigal conceals his character when he calls himself open-handed. Often inordinate laxity is believed to be kindness, and unbridled anger passes as the virtue of spiritual zeal."

We've all seen "prophetic" preachers who are just angry

young men. Some who dally at men's breakfasts and women's coffees ("I just love to be with my people") are merely procrastinating necessary paper work. Others who lock themselves in their offices, scrutinizing commentaries ("Just honing my gift of teaching"), are simply avoiding hospital calls.

Euphemisms are another form of hypocrisy. Since real Christian leaders never get angry, we can go for months without calling it such. The chairman of the board has undermined my proposal for a new mid-week youth program. Afterwards, flushed with emotion, I say, "I'm not angry with the chairman, just concerned about the youth." Or "I'm just grieved for the chairman's attitude." Or "I'm burdened for the future of the church." Right.

Euphemisms quickly slide into lying. In a sermon, I say, "I just read *Prayer* by Richard Foster, and he says . . ." — in fact, I skimmed only the first and last chapter searching for a sermon quote.

I say, "I couldn't reach you today" — actually I never tried, so of course I couldn't.

I say, "I think you would make a wonderful fifth-grade Sunday school teacher" — I really mean "You'd make a wonderful, warm-bodied babysitter for a class I'm desperate to staff."

The pressures to be holy, to lead righteously are so enormous that we sometimes start practicing a double standard — the ultimate form of hypocrisy. Jay Kesler tells a familiar story.

In the early years of his ministry, he noticed, many of his colleagues preached publicly that Christians needed to adhere to strict standards of conduct. They proclaimed rules without exceptions. In private, however, these same speakers acknowledged the difficulties if not impossibility of living up to the standards they preached.

"I noticed that when leaders like this got together and felt they could relax with one another, their conversation made it clear they felt laypeople couldn't handle the truth."

He tells a story of a speaker at a youth convention who gave a well-reasoned sermon, arguing that the Bible is without error not only when it talks about faith, but also when it speaks about history, geography, science, or any subject. The speaker didn't qualify the statement, and he allowed for no exceptions.

Later in a small-group session with leaders of the conference, the speaker was asked if you could really claim the Bible is authoritative on all scientific matters. The speaker replied by talking about the parable of the mustard seed, which Jesus described as "smaller than all the seeds that are upon the ground" (Mark 4:31).

"We know, of course," the speaker said, "that a mustard seed is not the smallest seed. The celery seed is smaller. We know that. You have to use common sense when you read the Bible. God is just saying in that parable that a very small thing becomes a very big thing."

The group sat in stunned silence, says Kesler. The speaker apparently didn't realize he had contradicted what he had argued for in his sermon. Suddenly, there were qualifications and exceptions.

Afterward, Kesler asked the speaker about the apparent contradiction. "You cannot tell the general population those kinds of things," the speaker said. "If common people feel you have doubts about one part of the Bible, they might perceive the Bible as not accurate."

Kesler concludes, "Many clergy feel that part of the 'holy' side of their calling is to pose as an authority figure, to state things categorically even when they themselves have questions and doubts." Others proclaim a tithe and only give 5 percent ("But my whole life is given to God"). Others condemn gambling and then buy lottery tickets ("Well, it's not as if I'm poor and can't afford it; it's just a harmless diversion for me").

The Greatest of These

The other spiritual sin is pride. Like hypocrisy, pride often looks and feels like commitment, devotion, and sacrifice for the kingdom; like hypocrisy, self-righteousness takes many wily forms.

Holier than them. Everybody is equal — nobody is really better than anyone else; nobody is really worse than anyone else. All have sinned and come short of the glory of God.

Or so we say. Most of us would be hard pressed to admit we

think we're better than others, but a lot of us do.

Sometimes we think we're better than parishioners. One October, our worship committee meeting began on a sour note: the senior pastor of our Southern California church fumed while he waited for tardy committee members. The Los Angeles Dodgers were battling in the World Series, and the committee members were — he just knew it — catching the last innings of game three.

"These people!" he sighed to me, an intern at the time. "I like baseball as well as the next guy, but if I can take the trouble to be here on time, they can too."

In a few minutes, the members drifted in, chattering about this hit and that catch. "Do you mind if we get started now?" the pastor snapped.

This incident and others convinced me this pastor thought himself superior to his parishioners. He tried to be patient with his parishioners' interests in sports and crocheting and drag racing, but it was clear that since his priorities were kingdom priorities, he was more committed to Christ than they were.

I looked down on this pastor (snubbing the spiritual snob!) until I became a pastor. Members went skiing on winter weekends; they chose the garden club over prayer meetings; they thought themselves sacrificial when they tithed 2 percent of their income. Some days, I was furious.

Noticing the difference in commitment isn't the problem; it's getting angry about it that signals self-righteousness. Most pastors are, in fact, more committed than church members to the church, and for good reasons: one, they wouldn't have entered the pastorate otherwise; two, pastors get paid to eat, sleep, and breathe the church.

In the course of my ministry, then, I noticed people's lesser commitment, and my usual response was understanding ("These people have their own callings, and being on this committee is just one facet"), and compassion ("I bet after working a full day, it's no fun to come to a church meeting").

When I became angry about the difference, that should have signaled a problem in me, not them. And the problem, more times than not, was self-righteousness.

I also noticed a holier-than-them attitude creeping within me when I thought about my colleagues in ministry.

In my first call, I served as an associate pastor of the largest Protestant church in the city. Without my knowing it, I began to equate the social dynamics of my setting (dynamic demographics, oodles of programs, sophisticated parishioners) with the spiritual dynamics of ministry.

I once took a drive to the country and passed through a small, small town with only one church. I was depressed as I left and tried to figure out why. I discovered I pitied the pastor of that church. He ministered to the same, simple people for years on end (no one was moving into this community!). He could offer few dynamic programs to his tiny congregation. He had no hope of church growth. *How does he keep himself motivated for ministry here?* I wondered. *Poor guy.*

It took me a few years — and a move to a small church — to realize how patronizing I had been. I couldn't imagine that ministry could be effective except based on my suburban assumptions. Unfortunately, I felt I was on the cutting edge of Jesus' work in the world. Pity the rest of the church.

Since then, I've become more sensitive to the patronizing comments of pastors of large churches: "Ah, yes. My favorite years in ministry were when I served that rural church in Sycamore, Illinois." (Then why didn't you stay in small-church ministry?)

"The pressures in the large church are so enormous. Sometimes I long for the simple days of pastoring a smaller church." (Ergo: "Now I'm sophisticated and adult-like, and someday you will be too, if you work as hard as I do.")

"I admire those brothers and sisters who labor in the small vineyards without much recognition." (In other words, "You're good little pastors.")

I once interviewed a pastor of a large church whose view of small-church pastors ("Bless their hearts. I love them," he said repeatedly) could be summarized in three words: *those poor jerks.*

After my move to a small church, though, I noticed the opposite self-righteous dynamic take effect. Suddenly, pastors of large churches were success driven; they were infatuated with numbers and graphs and indifferent to people and their spiritual needs; they strove to build organizations rather than kingdom communities. Etcetera, etcetera. I, of course, ministered out of purer motives.

Regardless of size of church, we're pretty good at finding ways to put ourselves above others. This is an especially strong temptation when we hear that another pastor has fallen morally, let's say, committing adultery. Our initial reaction is shock: "I can't believe it! How could he have done that? He seemed like a man of integrity."

For some, this is the healthy shock of recognition. Just as another's death suddenly reminds us of our mortality, another's adultery dramatizes our moral weakness. When a colleague falls, some of us fall to our knees, begging God to keep us from such sins.

For others, shock comes because a mentor has fallen. They may be saying, "I thought better of this colleague, who I've always looked up to." This may lead to a new appreciation of the doctrine of sin. Or it may lead, as it did for me once, to despising the fallen mentor: "All these years I looked up to him while he was doing that. That fraud!" In my bitterness, I assumed I would never do such a thing.

For others still, shock is an act, especially if a prominent minister has fallen. Underneath the righteous facade runs a smug and triumphant jealousy, which somehow justifies our relative righteousness. I know whereof I speak. The old moral insight remains valid: hearing of others' more blatant evils tends to make us feel good. Unfortunately, this is especially true of those whose very identity and calling are tied to living holy lives.

Possessor of gnosis. Pastors spend a lot of time with knowledge, with truth. We read about the doctrine of God's sovereignty; we ponder biomedical ethics; we scrutinize the revelations in Holy Scripture. You would think that an intense acquaintance with truth would nurture humility. Sometimes it does, often it doesn't.

Helmut Thielicke, the great German theologian and pastor, speaks of the dark side of knowledge when he addressed students of theology:

"Truth seduces us very easily into a kind of joy of possession: I have comprehended this and that, learned it, understood it. Knowledge is power. I am therefore more than the other man who does not know this and that. I have greater possibilities and also greater temptations. Anyone who deals with truth — as we theologians certainly do — succumbs all too easily to the psychology of the possessor. But love is the opposite of the will to possess. It is self-giving. It boasteth not itself, but humbleth itself."

Though this temptation is stronger in the early years of ministry, I'm not convinced we're ever through with it. It doesn't help that church members defer to you when, in casual conversation, the subject concerns the Bible, morality, or theology: "Pastor, you're the expert. What do you think?" Nor does it help that, in fact, we know a lot more about these "sacred" subjects than do our people. We're acquainted with truths that should make living the Christian life easier.

Again, it's not the fact of our superior knowledge that's the problem, but the posture we assume as a result. Take a related example: table manners. It bothers me to eat with a man who chews with his mouth open. If I'm loving, my attitude is, *He doesn't know what he's doing. I wonder how I can gently tell him.* If I'm haughty, I think, *Boy, is this guy a slob!* When it comes to spiritual knowledge, our congregations can become to us either lost sheep who need a gentle shepherd or stupid goats who just don't know any better.

Worse still is to use knowledge as a weapon, to show people, especially opponents, their utter ignorance, at least compared to you. If someone tries to argue a fine point from Romans 9, I can trounce her with, "I see what you're saying. But C. K. Barrett wouldn't agree, nor would the great Ernst Kasemann. I will grant you that C. E. B. Cranfield is ambivalent here. But I think the most incisive argument comes from Karl Barth's classic theological commentary. . . ." Game, set, match.

Thielicke notes that here, "Truth is employed as a means to personal triumph and at the same time as a means to kill, which is in the starkest possible contrast with love. It produces a few years later that sort of minister who operates not to instruct but to destroy his church. And if the elders, the church, and the young people begin to groan, if they protest to the church authorities, and finally stay away from worship, this young man is still pharisaical enough not to listen one bit."

The Ground of All Ministry. Perhaps the most subtle form of self-righteousness is described by Eugene Peterson, in his book *The Unpredictable Plant*:

"In our ministerial vocation we embark on a career of creating, saving, and blessing on behalf of God. . . . It is compelling work: a world in need, a world in pain, friends and neighbors and strangers in trouble — and all of them in need of compassion and food, healing and witness, confrontation and consolation and redemption."

Because we are motivated by Christ, by his grace and forgiveness, because our goals are defined by kingdom values, it rarely occurs to us that in this spiritual work anything could go wrong. But something always does. For some reason, in our zeal to fulfill the agenda of our Savior, we forget our own need of daily salvation.

"At first it is nearly invisible, this split between our need of the Savior and our work for the Savior. We *feel* so good, so grateful, so *saved*. And these people around us are in such need. We throw ourselves recklessly into the fray."

Our ministries begin to deteriorate from there, says Peterson, so that it isn't long before we end up identifying our work with Christ's work, so much so "that Christ himself recedes into the shadows and our work is spotlighted at center stage. Because the work is so compelling, so engaging — so *right* — we work with what feels like divine energy. One day we find ourselves (or others find us) worked into the ground. The work may be wonderful, but we ourselves turn out to be not so wonderful, becoming cranky, exhausted, pushy, and patronizing in the process."

In substituting our power for the power of the Holy Spirit, our goals for the goals of Christ, our all-too-human work for the work of God, we've succumbed to pride — at its most subtle, perhaps, but also in its most malevolent disguise.

Graceful Attention

Hypocrisy and self-righteousness, then, are the special sins of ministry, so it shouldn't surprise us that these were the sins that most concerned Jesus. When he criticized religious leaders — really the only people he was severe with — he never chastised them for sloth or lust or greed. Instead, he pointed to their hypocrisy and pride, the dangerous sins.

Part of the reason they're dangerous, of course, is that spiritual sins are not easy to defeat. They cannot be attacked directly. The more we make humility our aim, for instance, the more we're tempted to become proud of the humility we attain. One step forward, two steps back.

There is a more excellent way. The key, at least according to the church's best spiritual guides through the centuries, is graceful attention to our souls. Some have called it *spiritual direction*, others *contemplation*. In any case, as Eugene Peterson notes, it's the antidote to pride, and its cousin hypocrisy: "The alternative to acting like gods who have no need of God is to become contemplative pastors."

Contemplation includes prayer and worship, but more centrally, it means taking time regularly to pay attention to what God is doing within and around us. To practice it effectively requires two things.

First, we need to find time to be alone, no small achievement for the modern pastor. Still, it is a minimum requirement. In his classic, *The Imitation of Christ*, Thomas à Kempis writes, "Whoever intends to come to an inward fixing of his heart upon God and to have the grace of devotion must with our Saviour Christ withdraw from the world. No man can safely mingle among people save he who would gladly be solitary if he could."

Later he adds, "Our Lord and his angels will draw near and abide with those who, for the love of virtue, withdraw themselves from their acquaintances and from their worldly friends. It is better that a man be solitary and take good heed of himself than that, forgetting himself, he perform miracles in the world."

Second, and even more critical, we need to practice a graceful contemplation. The spiritual direction required is not a compulsive rooting out of every deviant behavior. We don't want to shame ourselves for our sins, nor lecture ourselves never to do them again. Jesus did not come that we might enjoy brooding self-flagellation.

Besides, the spiritual sins are not conquered with gritted teeth. The harder we try to conquer them, in fact, the more we'll despair. A baseball player doesn't break out of a slump by swinging harder and harder.

Instead, contemplation, in the classic sense, is a *graceful* attention to our lives. For instance, let's say I've made a vow, as I often have, not to live a hurried life. I want to manage my days so I have time for prayer and for people, and for the many interruptions that may be divine opportunities.

A phone call one afternoon, though, leads me to teach my son's mid-week Bible study class. Sunday, I agree to join a task force planning the new Christian education wing. The next week, I promise a friend I'll help him move.

Soon, I've packed my schedule as I always pack my schedule. I find myself rising early not to pray but to get to work. I don't chat with co-workers but stay huddled in my office. At home, I snap at my children and am cool with my wife.

Then I remember: I wasn't going to do all this! So I start browbeating myself: "You idiot! How did you get talked into all these commitments? What were you thinking of? Now you're hurried, you're impatient, and you're angry. Some Christian!"

I've become impatient with my impatience, and angry with my anger. I had somehow imagined that I could, by a mere act of the will, in but a few weeks, conquer a lifelong pattern. That's pride multiplied.

Instead, graceful attention means gentle recognition, gentle because we're noticing something that a gracious God knew all along. Since he didn't condemn us for it, neither do we need to condemn ourselves:

"Well, Lord, I see I've packed my schedule again, and there is hardly time for prayer anymore, let alone the important people of my life. This was certainly foolish. Forgive me. Help me to sort out exactly why I do this. Help me to accept my foolishness and your grace."

Only when grace is the first and last word of contemplation, can the scars left by the spiritual sins be healed. James I. Packer, in his book, *Rediscovering Holiness*, writes, "Pride blows us up like balloons, but grace punctures our conceit and lets the hot, proud air out of our system. The result . . . is that we shrink, and end up seeing ourselves as less — less nice, less able, less wise, less good, less strong, less steady, less committed, less of a piece — than ever we thought we were. We stop kidding ourselves that we are persons of great importance to the world and to God. . . . We bow to events that rub our noses in the reality of our own weaknesses, and we look to God for strength quietly to cope."

Three Key Areas

Everything is up for graceful contemplation, for the omnipresent God can meet us anywhere in our lives. Here, though, are three areas worth examining regularly.

● *Language.* Since words are the pastor's main tools, pastors are wise to pay attention to how they use language, in everyday speech and in teaching and preaching. Habits of swearing or criticizing or gossip are certainly to be attended to. But more subtle things deserve attention.

Helmut Thielicke has a wise caution for teachers of the Word: "Do not assume as a matter of course that you believe whatever impresses you theologically and enlightens you intellectually. Otherwise suddenly you are believing no longer in Jesus Christ, but in Luther, or in one of your other theological teachers."

For a long time, Dietrich Bonhoeffer was more my Lord than Jesus Christ. At least I quoted him a lot more in public than I did Jesus. That should have signalled something to me.

If we serve sophisticated congregations, who might be skeptical of personal religious language, we may begin speaking about the gospel in abstract language. Thielicke notes that when this becomes a habit, "A completely new style of thinking steals over us. We no longer say, as the man of prayer does, 'Lord Jesus Christ, Thou hast promised,' but we say, 'The kerygma discloses to us this and that.' " We may impress people with our sophistication, but it won't help them meet Jesus.

On the other hand, we may find we use personal religious language to talk about mere personal preference. As a pastor, I justified many decisions and motions to the board with godly words.

"God is leading us to reach out to young marrieds" — actually, I wanted to reach out to newly marrieds because in our neighborhood it was the most efficient way to grow a small church, which I was slightly ashamed of serving because it was so small.

"God wants us to look deep into our hearts to see what we should give to the church this year" — actually, I was anxious we weren't going to make budget, and that I wouldn't get a raise.

It's a common sin among pastors, either to take God out of or add him to conversations, depending on what will serve our interests. A steady, calm attention to our language alerts us to this subtle sin.

● *Pastoral activities.* In *The Minister and His Own Soul*, Thomas Hamilton Lewis, writes, "The minister's daily routine, so comforting, so helpful, so blessed to his people, may be his own spiritual vampire. The surgeon becomes increasingly insensible to suffering in his intentness upon removing it. And that is well for the surgeon and for us. But it is not well for a minister to become dulled in his spiritual sensibilities by ministering so constantly to keep alive the sensibilities of others."

The most troublesome state comes when a pastor, "praying so much for others finds his prayers not moving his own soul, preaching so much to others and bringing no message to his own soul, serving constantly at the altar and failing 'to offer up sacrifices first for his own sins.' "

As a fresh graduate from seminary, having just arrived in the community I was to serve, I met the local Episcopal priest. I was taken aback.

He denigrated preaching: "Don't get your hopes up, young man. It doesn't make much difference."

He made fun of one of his parishioners in the hospital: "Maybe he'll learn a little humility."

He made jokes about Communion, which I won't repeat.

As I was to discover, he was a pastor who administered efficiently the many programs of his church. He visited his people regularly in the hospital. He was a fine preacher. But he had pastored so long, had done these holy tasks so often, he was oblivious to the sacredness of his calling.

Pastors spend a lot of time with the holy: reading the Bible, performing baptisms, serving Communion, praying here, there, and everywhere. The old adage applies: familiarity breeds contempt, more so when it comes to handling things holy.

The only way to throttle familiarity is to pay attention afresh to what has become familiar. Many pastors, therefore, periodically use their own messages to inventory their spiritual lives, or their denomination's prayer books and liturgies as devotional guides. Others meditate on the sacramental elements of water, or wine and bread. Others contemplate the mystery of words, how such intangible things can connect people and God.

● *God's presence.* When we start paying attention to what is going on in and around us, we start to become aware of God. All contemplation is, in the end, a fresh discovery of God's activity in one's life.

"Spiritual direction is the act of paying attention to God, calling attention to God, being attentive to God in a person or circumstance or situation," writes Eugene Peterson. "A prerequisite is standing back, doing nothing. It opens a quiet eye of adoration. It releases the energetic wonder of faith. It notices the Invisibilities in and beneath and around the Visibilities. It listens for the Silences between the spoken Sounds."

One warm summer night, I lay awake, restless and lonely for my wife and children, who were away. Rather than picking up a book or writing or watching late-night TV, my first three lines of defense, I went outside and lay on our lawn. I started to pray but then decided just to pay attention to what was going on around me.

I decided to look up. I spend most my day just looking at my level and below. I see doors and windows and people and cars and the bottom half of buildings. So I consciously tilted my head and looked up. I saw the branches of our maple tree swaying, swaying against a sky dotted with a thousand stars.

I decided to listen. I spend most of my day in my head,

listening to my own agenda whirl away, or at best, hearing the words of others. Now I listened to the wind, to rustling leaves, swooshing, brushing, rushing here and there.

I decided to feel, which I rarely have time to do. The warm air glided over my skin. Grass tickled my neck. Firm ground pressed against my back.

Suddenly, and for no more than a few seconds, mystery and beauty were manifest. The universe seemed so fragile, like a glass ornament, yet so wonderful, like a best present of all. I felt insignificant. Yet love pulsed, through me, around me. The glory of God. I lay there for many minutes, nearly in tears.

I relate this experience not because it's unusual, but precisely because it is so very usual. Not that it happens to us everyday, but most Christians have had these little epiphanies. The great spiritual teachers of the church tell us that though we cannot control such encounters, we can lead lives — of graceful attention — that can prepare us and make possible such epiphanies.

Paying attention is, then, more than an exercise in moral vigilance. It is not the making of resolutions and willful activity. It is mostly making room for God, and thus, making room for love. The first commandment is not to obey God or to be righteous. It is to love God, which means first to be loved by him.

Only then will we have the courage to contemplate our hypocrisy and gently probe the pride that snakes its way into our souls. Only then will we obtain eyes to see God in, with, and under us, even the ugly us. Only this love makes the moral demands of ministry bearable, even joyful.

"Love is a great and good thing," writes Thomas à Kempis, "and alone makes heavy burdens light and bears in equal balance things pleasing and displeasing. . . . The noble love of Jesus perfectly imprinted in man's soul makes a man do great things, and stirs him always to desire perfection and to grow more and more in grace and goodness."

In the end, the right, reasonable, and ridiculous call to pastoral holiness is mostly the call to know and share this love.

To truly care for people requires not caring too much about their approval or disapproval.

— John Ortberg

CHAPTER TWO

Breaking the Approval Addiction

Mayor Richard J. Daley, who was as celebrated in Chicago for his malapropisms as for his ability to get votes out of corpses, once said of his opponents, "They have vilified me, they have crucified me, yes, they have even criticized me."

His honor could have been speaking for those of us in ministry. Whether it's politics or the pastorate, not everyone will believe we're wonderful.

Criticism, especially "friendly fire," can kill our motivation and energy. Generally we pastors have a fairly high need to be liked. While not a bad thing, the need for strokes can set us up to have difficulty dealing with criticism.

But if the actions of Jesus and the prophets are any indication, then giving effective spiritual leadership will surely mean doing things that displease the very people whose approval we desire. For most of us, it's only a matter of time (and usually not very much time) before the people we're supposed to serve have vilified, crucified, or even criticized us.

Our strong reaction to such criticism reveals, I believe, a serious addiction problem. It has nothing to do with substance abuse or chemical dependency. It is, rather, a craving for approval.

Diagnosis

Its primary symptom is the tendency to confuse my "performance in ministry" with my worth as a person, to seek the kind of approval from people that can only satisfy when it comes from God.

This addiction has been around at least as long as the church. Paul thunders against it to the Galatians: "Am I now trying to win the approval of men, or of God? If I were still trying to please men, I would not be a servant of Christ."

Even more disturbing is the diagnosis from John about people who were blocked from faith because of this addiction: "They loved praise from men more than praise from God."

Addiction shows up in odd ways and at unwelcome times.

It was four o'clock in the morning. I lay awake. I had recently left a secure job with a real church to plant a new one, with no buildings, no offices, no secretaries, no handbell choirs, no professional scaffolding at all, and only six weeks worth of expenses (including my salary) in the bank. I do some of my best worrying at 4:00 A.M.

Something disturbs me about this particular concern, however. It occurs to me that a good chunk of my apprehension over this venture is not just that if we don't succeed, many people will not meet God, although that's part of it. My anxiety is not just over the financial needs of a family with three small, ravenous children; if worse comes to worse I can fall back on a degree in psychology. (There will always be enough rich, neurotic people to counsel.)

Part of the fear nagging at my heart — a bigger part than I want to admit — is that if the church doesn't succeed, I won't look successful.

Recognition, paradoxically, is the first step towards liberation. At least when I become aware of my need to appear successful, I can say, "I refuse to make decisions or hold back on risks based on something as stupid as my need to impress people who most likely are not even thinking about me anyway. I refuse to allow the approval or disapproval of others to determine my worth as a person."

But recognition doesn't make it go away.

The Voices Within

When I get up to speak on Sunday morning, the congregation hears my voice, but I hear another, more confusing voice in my head. It's also my voice. Sometimes it shouts, *Thus saith the Lord!* But at other times, more often than I care to admit, the voice is less prophetic.

What will they think of me? the voice wonders.

Sometimes I feel less like the prophet Amos and more like Sally Field at the Academy Awards. I find myself desperate to be able to say as she did when she'd won her second Oscar: "You like me! You really like me!"

I do not like this Sally Field voice. I wish I had more of a Rhett Butler voice and could greet evaluations at the door with, "Frankly, my dear, I don't give a . . . rip."

When Jesus spoke, he was free from the need to create an impression, free to speak the truth in love. But the voice within me is not free. It is driven by ego and pride. It is ugly to me, and I'd turn it off if I could, but turning it off proves not to be so simple. Where does this voice come from?

In *Lake Wobegon Days*, Garrison Keillor writes about growing up without praise under the theory that compliments cause swelled heads. But the years of emotional malnourishment, far from weaning him away from the need for approval, instead created an insatiable appetite for it:

"Under this thin veneer of modesty lies a monster of greed. I drive away faint praise, beating my little chest, waiting to be named Sun-God, King of America, Idol of Millions, Bringer of Fire, The Great Haji, Thun-Dar the Boy Giant. I don't want to say, 'Thanks, glad you liked it.' I want to say, 'Rise, my people. Remove your faces from the carpet, stand, look me in the face.' "

This, however, would make for a rather awkward benediction.

Approval and Anger

Sociologist George Herbert Meade wrote about the "generalized other," the mental representation we carry inside of that group by whose judgment we measure our success or failure. Our sense of esteem and worth is largely wrapped up in their appraisal of our work.

Your generalized other is a composite of all the Siskels and Eberts in your life whose thumbs up or thumbs down carries emotional weight. This may include parents, seminary professors, key lay leaders, or other pastors. My guess is that most of us in ministry have the same set of ego issues as people in any other profession. We just have a different way of keeping score.

When my identity is wrapped up in whether or not I am perceived as successful, I am set up for the approval addiction, for it is my very sense of self that is on the line.

"Who am I?" Henri Nouwen asks. "I am the one who is liked, praised, admired, disliked, hated, or despised. Whether I am a pianist, a businessman, or a minister, what matters is how I am perceived by my world."

And when my drug of choice is withheld, I respond with the same anger as any other addict: *Don't these people know I have the best interests of the church at heart? Don't they know I could have gone into some other profession and made lots more money?* It's as if I'm entitled to universal trust and consideration.

Wherever it comes from, whenever my craving for approval

makes itself known, I'd better pay attention.

One Sunday morning, as I was greeting people at the door, a visitor handed me his card.

"I usually attend Hollywood Presbyterian," he said, "but we're visiting here today. Give me a call sometime."

I looked down at his card — SPEECH INSTRUCTOR.

Hollywood Presbyterian is the home of Lloyd Ogilvie. Lloyd Ogilvie is perfect. His hair is perfect, his robe is perfect, his smile is perfect, but above all, his voice is perfect. Deep as the ocean, rich and resonant, Lloyd Ogilvie sounds like what I expect God sounds like on a really good day.

Next to his voice, mine sounds like I'm in perpetual adolescence. It's difficult to feel prophetic when you hear yourself chirping like Mickey Mouse, "Okay, now, let's repent."

When I catch myself comparing myself to others or thinking, *I could be happy if only I had what they have*, then I know I need to withdraw for a while and listen for another voice. Away from the winds, earthquakes, and fires of human recognition, I can again hear the still, small voice, posing the question it always asks of self-absorbed ministers: *What are you doing here?*

I reply by whining about some of my Ahabs and Jezebels. And the voice gently reminds me, as it has reminded thousands of Elijahs before me, that I am only a small part of a much larger movement, and at the end of the day there is only one king whose approval will matter.

The voice also whispers, *Do not despise your place, your gifts, your voice, for you cannot have another's, and it would not fulfill you if you could.*

Celebrating Solitude

To truly care *for* people requires not caring too much *about* their approval or disapproval. Otherwise the temptation to give their preferences too much emotional weight is almost inevitable.

To lead people effectively, without being damaged in the process, requires regular withdrawal from the very people I'm trying to lead.

Thomas Merton wrote that the desert fathers considered society to be a shipwreck from which all individuals must swim for their lives. The very pecking orders and ladders of success I naturally find myself climbing they fled in horror.

In solitude I see that career successes and failures, which look so huge in my day-to-day life, take on a much smaller look from an eternal perspective. ("If you can meet with triumph and disaster," Kipling wrote, "treat those two impostors both the same.") And the development of my soul, which I can lose sight of altogether in my routine strivings, is revealed as the one great task of my life.

Approval addiction involves some irrational thought processes, which solitude helps clear. Psychiatrist David Burns notes it is not another person's approval or compliment that makes me feel good, it is *my belief* that there is validity to the compliment.

Suppose you were to visit a psychiatric ward, he imagines, and a patient approaches you: "You are wonderful. I had a vision from God. He told me the thirteenth person to walk through the door would be the Special Messenger. You are the thirteenth, so I know you are God's Chosen One, the Prince of Peace, the Holy of Holies. Let me kiss your shoe."

Most likely your self-esteem-o-meter would not rise. Why not? Because between other people's approval and your pleasure in it is your assessment of the validity of their approval.

You are not the passive victim of others' opinions. In fact, their opinions are powerless until you validate them. No one's approval will affect me unless I grant it credibility and status. The same holds true for disapproval.

Several years back, at a previous church, I used to get regular complaints from a parishioner about all aspects of the service, mostly that the music was too loud. When he couldn't get satisfaction from me, he hounded other staff and board members.

One afternoon my secretary informed me that I had a visitor from OSHA, the federal watchdog agency. It turned out this same parishioner, as a last resort, asked for government assistance to get the sound system turned down on Sunday mornings. By law, OSHA was required to send someone out.

"Can you imagine the kind of ridicule I've taken all week," the OSHA representative said, apologetically, "with people knowing I'm going out to bust a church?"

Though dramatically stated and strongly disapproving, these complaints didn't bother me at all. They originated from a character who lived on the fringe, as far as I was concerned.

I realized from this incident that no one's disapproval can emotionally affect me without my authorization. For me to allow disapproval to subtract from my sense of worth as a human being is both irrational and destructive.

Getting Guidance

In addition to solitude, I find it helpful to have another person or two to whom I regularly go for guidance on these issues.

Some time ago, I heard from an attender that our church doesn't talk enough about sin.

"Can you imagine that?" I said later to one of my spiritual guides in my non-defensive, emotionally open way. "What he really wants is a sermon series promoting the legalistic, superficial, developmentally arrested approach to morality that will condemn outsiders and reinforce his own self-righteous smugness!"

I waited for my friend to agree with me that this guy had obviously fixated at Kohlberg's lowest stage of moral development (preconventional level — heteronomous morality).

Instead he asked me two pointed questions:

"Well, *do* you preach about sin enough?"

Then, after I squirmed, he added, "And what is this need you have for everybody to agree with everything you do?"

He forced me to reexamine my own understanding of sin and to proclaim it in a clearer way. He also reminded me that ministry is not about getting people to like me.

Having a few such people in my life helps me answer a practical question: How do I know when I need to respond to criticism and disapproval? What would suggest that more is at stake than whether a parishioner likes or dislikes me?

To Cope or Confront?

A certain amount of discontent is inevitable, and probably even healthy, in any group. Not every infection calls for a massive dose of penicillin. Many of the personal hits a pastor takes will be absorbed in the natural flow of events.

But at least two types of situations call for criticism to be confronted and refuted.

One is if the criticism affects the health of the body of Christ.

I have a friend who pastors with as much sensitivity and integrity as anyone I know. Because of several changes going on in the church, however, he was accused of (among other things) being a megalomaniac. This has about as much validity as charging Mr. Rodgers with inciting violence.

This criticism, however, went far beyond what his psyche could tolerate. It struck directly at his ability to serve the church effectively; it threatened the church's ability to choose and follow its leaders. Because it affected the health of the church, this attack had to be handled head on.

The other time I probably need to respond directly to criticism is when the criticism keeps nagging away at me.

At one point early in my ministry, we had a particularly difficult EGR ("extra-grace required," as Carl George calls them) person on the governing board. When his term finally expired, I breathed a prayer of thanks.

Sometime later I was engaged in what was supposed to be an extended time of prayer, when I realized I was deep into an anger fantasy involving this former board member. In my anger fantasies, I never torture my opponents too brutally, because then I would feel guilty (and that would rob my sense of revenge of its purity). Usually in my fantasies, whomever I'm angry at suddenly realizes with painful, shame-ridden clarity the massive, unfair hurt they've inflicted on me and my family.

"I hope you're satisfied with what you've done," I always say, pouring hot coals upon their too-late-repentant heads until they feel like scum.

"I hope when you go home and look in the mirror tonight you can live with what you see."

It occurred to me that I might still be angry with this man. I realized then I needed to meet with him and discuss it, even if all the issues didn't get resolved (they didn't).

The Discipline of Secrecy

We have yet another weapon in the battle against the approval addiction: the discipline of secrecy.

"Be careful not to practice your 'acts of righteousness' before men to be seen by them," Jesus warned. "If you do, you will have no reward from your Father in heaven."

His particular examples relate to financial contributions, fasting, and prayer, but they reflect a deep insight into all of human nature. I used to think Jesus meant God had a reward stored up for me in heaven, but if my motives were self-serving, I would lose it. What he's really talking about, however, is losing the intrinsic power of these good deeds to help me enter the life of the kingdom now. He was talking to people who were addicted to having their righteousness admired — so addicted, it was impossible for them to enjoy righteousness for its own sake.

If I give my money away, I have less opportunity to become a slave to it, and I can experience true freedom and joy. If I choose to impress people by making sure they know about my generosity, however, the nature of my action changes. I settle for the narcotic of approval, and instead of becoming a little more free, I become a little more enslaved.

On one particularly busy morning at our house, I voluntarily emptied the dishwasher before my wife got up, even though it wasn't in *my* job description. That evening, when she still hadn't commented on it, I tactfully commented on how fortunate she was to have such a thoughtful husband.

At this point, the fundamental character of what I had done was altered. Instead of one tiny action helping me become more like Christ, more like a servant without feeling I had done something extraordinary, it became one more item on a *quid pro quo* checklist.

Jesus says to do good things without telling anybody about it. Eventually we'll find we lose the need to let people know. And we'll also find we can do good because it really is the most liberating, joyful way to live.

I try to implement this discipline of secrecy regularly in my own life. If I'm going to a meeting where there will be people I perceive as important (my "generalized others"), I try ahead of time to identify the things I'll be tempted to say to impress them, and I declare those topics off limits. (I don't get carried away with it, though. You notice this article didn't get published anonymously.)

Weaning myself from the approval of others is a lifetime project. Its vise-like grip on my soul can be broken, however, enabling me, when vilified, crucified, and even criticized, to rest in the approval of the One I serve.

We are not tempted to do bad things as much as we are tempted to try things God has not called us to do.

— Richard Exley

CHAPTER THREE

Taming Ambition

I n August of 1976, a jury found the Reverend Charles Blair, pastor of the 6,000-member Calvary Temple in Denver, Colorado, guilty of seventeen counts of fraud and illegal sale of securities. Blair had raised $14 million from about 3,400 investors to finance the church's ill-fated geriatric center.

Blair was fined $12,750 and placed on five years probation, but he was allowed to remain as pastor of Calvary Temple. Under his leadership the church was able to repay the investors according to a plan approved by the bankruptcy court.

From all reports, Charles Blair is a man of integrity, a conclusion reinforced by his commitment to repay every investor. No evidence suggests he, or his family, benefited in any way from the illegal sale of securities. Though Blair knowingly allowed financially troubled investors to invest in the Life Center, nothing suggests he intended to defraud them.

All of which makes this scenario more troubling: this is not the story of an evil man reaping the wages of sin but the tragic account of a good man whose vision exceeded his judgment.

In reflecting on the testimony about Blair's financial and religious empire, Gerald H. Quick, one of the twelve jurors who found him guilty, said, "Maybe the Rev. Charles Blair should stick to preaching and stay out of the securities business. . . . Maybe ambition got in the way of his common sense."

Was ambition, the drive to succeed, the culprit? Perhaps. Yet without ambition nothing of significance is ever achieved. How can we make ambition our servant rather than our master? Or as one person put it, how can we tame our "drum-major instincts"?

What's the Source?

In his book, *The Man Who Could Do No Wrong*, Blair candidly confesses his mistakes and their source. Growing up during the Great Depression left him with a deep-seated self-doubt and a burning desire to succeed. No one would ever again look down on him, he determined, nor would his children ever endure the bitter humiliation that characterized his childhood. Consequently he was ever conscious of his public image. He drove the right kind of car, wore the best suits, and fraternized with the right people.

This inordinate concern for his public image, coupled with his enormous success, made it nearly impossible for him to distinguish between the voice of God and his own subconscious ego needs. While his desire to provide a center for the handicapped and the aged was noble, it was not necessarily birthed by God.

Herein lies the difference between godly and human ambition: godly ambition originates in the heart of the Father and is fueled by a sincere desire to please him; human ambition originates in the heart of people and is driven by their own ego needs.

A classic example of well-intended but misguided human ambition is found in 2 Samuel 7. King David had finally established his throne in Jerusalem and was, at long last, free from military conflict. One day he said to Nathan the prophet, " 'Here I am, living in a palace of cedar, while the ark of God remains in a tent.' Nathan replied to the king, 'Whatever you have in mind, go ahead and do it, for the Lord is with you' " (2 Sam. 7:2–3).

Unfortunately neither David nor Nathan had sought the counsel of the Lord. Apparently they did not think it was necessary. Building a temple seemed only logical. And herein lies a great danger to the man or woman of God: we are not tempted to do bad things as much as we are tempted to try things God has not called us to do.

Still, if we are sensitive to the Holy Spirit, the Lord will "check" us before we get in over our heads. That's what God did for King David. According to 2 Samuel 7:4, the word of the Lord came to Nathan that very night, telling David not to build the temple. Following this divine revelation, Nathan faced that moment dreaded by all advisers to powerful men — to stand in opposition to David's plan. His initial support of David's desire only complicated matters.

Had Nathan been more self-serving and less obedient, he might have ignored this word and let David go ahead with his plans. By the same token, had David been more ambitious, he might have resented Nathan's counsel and rejected it to his own sorrow. He was spared the painful humiliation that befalls so many spiritual leaders who ignore the counsel of wise friends.

Blair admits he dismissed the warning signals, seeing them as obstacles to be overcome by faith. For example, he ignored the concerns expressed by his wife, Betty; they were not one in heart and mind. He said he never submitted his dream to the counsel of others, so he could never say, "It seemed good to the Holy Spirit and to us" (Acts 15:28).

Though we can never be absolutely sure a vision we pursue is from God, we can minimize the risk of making a mistake. First, we can practice a ruthless honesty with ourselves, daily admitting our ambition, reminding ourselves that we must not make important decisions without others' counsel.

Second, we can become skeptical of our motives. I've developed the practice of asking myself some hard questions:

1. Have I fully surrendered this desire to the Lord?

2. Is this truly God's plan or just my own ambition?

3. Am I waiting for the Lord to "open the door" or am I impatiently forcing things to happen?

4. Am I resorting to human methods in an attempt to accomplish God's plan?

5. Am I attempting this because God has called me to do it or because I am driven to succeed?

Admittedly, these are subjective questions, but with steady attention to our souls, we can grow in our ability to discern our motives. Still, even if I satisfactorily answer these questions, I do not trust my conclusions. Jeremiah said, "The heart is deceitful above all things. . . . Who can understand it?" (Jeremiah 17:9). Spiritual guidance, whether it comes in the form of an inner witness or through a personal vision, is simply too subjective to be left to my judgment. I must submit my vision to the scrutiny of godly advisers. Only if it passes muster with them can I move ahead with confidence.

"Nothing is more dangerous," writes Richard Foster, "than leaders accountable to no one. We all need others who can laugh at our pomposity and prod us into new forms of obedience. Power is just too dangerous a thing for any of us to face alone."

Called or Driven?

While serving as pastor of Christian Chapel, I oversaw the field education of several seminarians who served our congregation. Well do I remember the day one of them shared a paper on ministry. In it he referred to Jesus as a "driven man," consumed with his ministry. A truly committed minister, according to this student's thinking, would be a "driven man," willing to sacrifice everything on the altar of "his" ministry.

As he read his paper, alarm bells went off in my head. When

he finished, he looked up for my response.

"Dave, I don't think Jesus was a driven man," I said carefully. "I believe the Scriptures portray him as a called man. A driven man is consumed with his own needs and desires. A called man is committed to the Father. A driven man is ambitious. A called man is obedient."

The expression on his face suggested this was a new thought for him. He had been reared on slogans like, "Make no small plans here," and "Nothing succeeds like success!"

I picked a dog-eared copy of Gordon MacDonald's *Ordering Your Private World* from my bookcase and read him MacDonald's list of eight characteristics of driven people:

"1. A driven person is most often gratified only by accomplishment. . . . He becomes the sort of person who is always reading books and attending seminars that promise to help him to use what time he has even more effectively. Why? So that he can produce more accomplishments, which in turn will provide greater gratification.

"2. A driven person is preoccupied with the symbols of accomplishment. . . . That means that he will be aware of the symbols of status: titles, office size and location, positions on organizational charts, and special privileges.

"3. A driven person is usually caught in the uncontrolled pursuit of expansion. Driven people like to be a part of something that is getting bigger and more successful. . . . They rarely have any time to appreciate the achievements to date.

"4. Driven people tend to have a limited regard for integrity. . . . Shortcuts to success become a way of life. Because the goal is so important, they drift into ethical shabbiness. Driven people become frighteningly pragmatic.

"5. Driven people often possess limited or undeveloped people skills. . . . There is usually a 'trail of bodies' in the wake of the driven person. Of this person we are most likely to find ourselves saying, 'He is miserable to work with, but he certainly gets things done.'

"6. Driven people tend to be highly competitive. . . . Thus, he is likely to see others as competitors or as enemies who must be beaten — perhaps even humiliated — in the process.

"7. A driven person often possesses a volcanic force of anger.

"8. Driven people are usually abnormally busy. They are usually too busy for the pursuit of ordinary relationships in marriage, family, or friendship . . . not to speak of one with God."

This is not what Jesus was like, nor is it the kind of minister any of us want to become. Yet the ministry is filled with these kind of people. Most, I believe, entered ministry with pure motives, but in the course of time, ambition, often disguised as a godly vision, became their master.

We've all read fictitious accounts of people who made a pact with the devil, who in a moment sold him their souls in return for personal success. Reality is seldom like that: we lose our soul day by day, one piece at a time. We don't realize what is happening until it's too late. Selfish ambition eats away at us like unseen cancer, until one day we discover we've succumbed to the malignancy of ambition.

The Secret of Service

In his book, *It Doesn't Take a Hero*, General H. Norman Schwarzkopf, writes, "The Army, with its emphasis on rank and medals and efficiency reports, is the easiest institution in the world in which to get consumed with ambition. Some officers spend all their time currying favor and worrying about the next promotion — a miserable way to live. But West Point saved me from that by instilling the ideal of service above self — to do my duty for my country even if it brought no gain at all. It gave me far more than a military career — it gave me a calling."

Service above self — that's the secret of taming our ambition.

I learned this early in my ministry. The first congregation I served was small and riddled with petty jealousies. Like many small churches in rural areas, it was comprised of family members — parents and grandparents; children and grandchildren; aunts, uncles, and cousins. They didn't consider themselves cliquish and seemed anxious for the church to grow. But they were content with the status quo and resented the changes new families brought to the church.

Instead of reaching out to new converts, they were critical and judgmental, not only of new members but also of me. After my first year, things reached a boiling point. They accused me of ruining their church. Before I arrived, divorced people and single parents had not been a part of the church. Now they attended, and the established members didn't like it. There was talk about circulating a petition demanding my resignation.

At the time, I felt threatened and betrayed. I unwittingly raised the level of hostility; since I felt a personal responsibility to disciple the new converts, I spent most of my time ministering to them. The charter members felt ignored.

When things became desperate, I cried out to the Lord. Over a three-week period, I became convinced God was directing me to conduct an old-fashioned, foot-washing service. It made no sense to me, but my inner promptings seemed to grow stronger by the day.

The following Sunday morning, I announced that the evening service would be for men only. I immediately sensed the congregation grow uneasy. By the time I reached the parsonage after the service, the phone was ringing. It was Brother Hoover, an 84-year-old, long-time member of the church. He informed me that his wife had been attending church with him for more than sixty years and that if she was not welcome in the service, then he wasn't coming either.

Without giving me a chance to reply, he hung up. I was sick at heart. The Hoovers were one of the few families who weren't opposing me. Now I had offended them!

But it was too late to change my mind. That evening nine men sat on metal folding chairs, facing each other. They sat quietly, occasionally glancing toward the Communion table where I stood. I started the service by instructing the men to remove their shoes and socks. They looked at each other as if to say, *This kid has really lost his mind this time* (I was only 21). Still, they did as I requested, and in a matter of minutes two rows of barefooted men faced each other.

While the men were removing their shoes and socks, I took off my coat and rolled up my shirt sleeves. Picking up a basin of water and a towel, I faced them.

"Some of you feel I've played favorites," I said, "that I haven't ministered to your families as I should. You are justified in your feelings. But I want you to know any time I wronged you, I did it ignorantly, out of inexperience, never maliciously. As a demonstration of my sincere desire to serve you, in any way, great or small, I'm going to wash your feet."

I knelt before the man nearest me and said, "I apologize for any wrong I have done you, and I ask your forgiveness." Then I washed his feet. I repeated that act before each man.

During that simple ritual, something almost miraculous took place. By taking a towel and a basin of water, by getting down on my knees, by washing their feet and apologizing, I had disarmed those men. I defused their anger. When I made myself vulnerable, when I placed myself in their hands, at their mercy, I appealed to the love and goodness in their hearts.

That experience also radically changed me. Until that service, I had assumed ministers, especially evangelists, were sanctified celebrities. The church existed to fulfill our agendas. As a result, I noticed every slight, however insignificant. I felt unappreciated and was constantly unhappy.

God's answer for my ambition was a basin of water and a towel, especially the attitude of loving service to others.

Holy Ambition

For years I found myself trapped in the vicious cycle of competition. My predominant concern was "How can I build a bigger church?" rather than "How can I be a more faithful minister of Jesus Christ?" The determining factor in my decision making was not, "Is this God's will?" but "How will this look on my resume?"

I sincerely cared about the people God had entrusted to my care, and I endeavored to be a good pastor. But always lurking in the shadows of my soul was my personal ambition.

But I was frustrated because I knew I couldn't compete. In a system in which a minister's value was measured by the numbers — baptisms, budget, and buildings — I was outclassed. For the first fourteen years of ministry, I served small churches (under 100 members) in remote rural areas. Nothing I accomplished could compare with the success of city pastors.

In addition, it seemed I was always looking up to see some minister whiz by in the fast lane. His achievements dwarfed mine, making mine seem despairingly insignificant.

I managed to deal with my relative insignificance as long as I remained isolated in my own pastorate. I became troubled, however, whenever I attended a district meeting or a national conference. The featured speakers were always "successful" pastors. In their presence, I felt like a nobody. I often found their achievements intimidating rather than inspiring.

Since most of them were several years my senior, I rationalized that by the time I reached their age I would be equally successful. I was jealous when a classmate or someone younger than me was the featured speaker.

At one General Council of my denomination, a peer of mine was a featured speaker. I had to admit he was committed, gifted, and articulate. Still I picked his message apart while 14,000 worshipers hung on his every word. Inwardly I seethed. The better he preached the more jealous I became.

For weeks afterward, I alternated between anger and depression. Envy was eating a hole in my soul. Jealousy was making me sick. Finally I confessed to God my sinful feelings and my inability to subdue them. I confessed my feelings of failure and inadequacy. Gently the Lord comforted me.

Slowly I learned a new way of determining my self-worth. I didn't have to measure myself against the achievements of more successful ministers. Instead of the numbers game, over which I had only the slightest control, I learned to base my success on my relationship with Jesus. With God's help I set new goals — character and spiritual goals. From that day forward, I determined to measure my success only by my obedience to Jesus Christ and my willingness to allow the Holy Spirit to conform me to the image of God's Son.

For the first time in my life, I felt liberated. The work of the ministry still needed to be done, but now it was the by-product of my relationship with the Lord, an expression of who I was in him, rather than an attempt to prove my worth. I felt content, rather than competitive, and for the first time rejoiced genuinely in the achievements of my peers.

While I served Christian Chapel in Tulsa, Oklahoma, the church experienced significant growth. I began to feel smug. God confronted me by impressing upon my heart this truth: "Richard, if you couldn't build your self-worth on the size of your congregation when it numbered less than 100 people, you can't do it now."

Such an attitude isn't easy and doesn't come naturally to me. I constantly battle against selfish ambition. Over and over I must submit myself to the sanctifying work of the Spirit.

I constantly aim to be what God has called me to *be*; that way I'm assured of accomplishing what God has called me to *do*. I'm discovering that human ambition, tamed and transformed, can become godly ambition. As we daily submit to the Lord in all things, we will grow in grace until "the things of earth grow strangely dim in the light of his glory and grace."

Sloth is the failure to do what needs to be done when it needs to be done.

— John Ortberg

CHAPTER FOUR

Confessions of a Lazy Pastor

The sloth is a tropical mammal that lives much of its life hanging upside-down from tree branches. When obliged to descend to the ground, sloths crawl along a level surface at the rate of ten feet a minute (meaning their top sprint is one-ninth of a mile per hour).

Sloths are generally sluggish and inactive; they build no nests and seek no shelter even for their young. They sleep fifteen to twenty-two hours a day, rising in the late afternoon to eat whatever leaves may be close at hand. Being so passive, they are virtually untrainable, although occasionally you'll find one working as a denominational official or on a roadside construction crew.

From time to time, a sloth hangs around my home and office, a discovery that has surprised me. I'm familiar with lots of my faults but never suspected this one. Up to now, I've been careful to whom I admit it.

I'm careful because sloth is our society's unforgivable sin. It is almost never mentioned. I can't remember the last time I heard anyone confess it.

Think of job interviews. When someone is asked, "What's your biggest weakness?" 90 percent of the answers are variations of "I work too hard," and "I tend to be too perfectionistic." When have you heard someone say, "I'm just too darn lazy"?

But I've discovered that I have to quit playing this game. Psychiatrist and best-selling author Scott Peck says that ultimately there is one great impediment to spiritual growth "and that is laziness. If we overcome laziness, all the other impediments will be overcome. If we do not overcome laziness, none of the others will be hurdled. . . . Spiritual growth is effortful, as we have been reminded again and again."

Here are some ways I've tried to make that effort and so deal with sloth.

Not Doing What Needs to Be Done

Sloth is deceptive and destructive. One reason people don't admit sloth is they don't recognize it.

In the past I would have considered anything but sloth to be one of my problems because I seem to be so busy. Sloth doesn't necessarily mean we're doing nothing. Sloth is the failure to do what needs to be done when it needs to be done — like the kamikaze pilot who flew seventeen missions.

I came gradually to the realization that this was a temptation. I would have a task I didn't look forward to — say, setting up an appointment to confront someone about a broken relationship. Suddenly, a myriad of other tasks leapt up and begged to be done. I would clean my desk, call a staff meeting, write two articles for a newsletter we didn't even publish.

I did a lot. But over time I discovered that all too often I didn't do what needed to be done when it needed to be done. Just as most alcoholics don't live on skid row, most sloth-aholics don't spend their days eating bon-bons and watching *The Young and the Restless*.

That's why Scott Peck notes that even workaholics can be lazy. They may work furiously but only because they are trying to avoid doing something truly needful.

Frederick Buechner, in his book *Wishful Thinking*, put it this way:

"A slothful man . . . may be a very busy man. He is a man who goes through the motions, who flies on automatic pilot. Like a man with a bad head cold, he has mostly lost his sense of taste and smell. He knows something's wrong with him, but not wrong enough to do anything about. Other people come and go, but through glazed eyes he hardly notices them. He is letting things run their course. He is getting through his life."

Unfortunately, too often that's been a description of me.

Signs of Sloth

When I have confessed my struggles in this area with a few carefully chosen confidants, their response — without exception — has been: "What? You, too? I thought I was the only one." Apparently we all struggle with our own secret forms of sloth. (I know only one person who I'm certain never struggles with laziness. He's four years old. We're hoping it hits him soon.)

Max De Pree, author of *Leadership Jazz*, wrote that one of the most difficult tasks of leadership is intercepting entropy, which he defined loosely as "everything has a tendency to deteriorate."

He listed signals of deterioration:

— relationships become superficial

— there is little time for celebration and ritual

— leaders try to control rather than liberate people

— day-to-day pressures push aside our need to envision and

plan goals

— there is a noticeable loss of grace, style, and civility in our conversations and lifestyles.

Typically the entropy I most need to intercept is my own. Sloth is like gravity; you have to deal with it every day. So I have learned to watch for six tell-tale signs that help me diagnose its presence:

1. My desk top and office get messier.

2. I run late.

3. I stop doing things my wife appreciates, say keeping the grass under three feet high. I've agreed to do it but find myself not doing it.

The problem is not energy. For example, after several marathon days — up before dawn, running non-stop until late — I may come home to a free evening but only have enough energy to drag myself down the hall and collapse in the chair. I'd like to help around the house, but I've given everything for the ministry.

Then the phone rings. I summon my last reserves to pick up the receiver. It's a good friend: several guys have gotten hold of a gym, and a basketball game starts in forty-five minutes.

What happens next is a miracle. Energy, strength, and vitality swarm back into my body like the swallows returning to Capistrano.

4. I find telephone messages I haven't returned since the Carter administration.

5. I experience an odd combination of hurry and wastefulness. I rush in the morning, telling my wife I have no time for breakfast, no time to see the kids off to school; too much to do. Later in the morning, I read the sports section or make an unnecessary phone call.

6. I have a sense of dis-ease at the end of the day: I just don't feel right about what I've done or been that day. When God created the world, he spent time at the end of each day reflecting on what he had done and finding a sense of rightness to it. "It was good," he said. Restedness flows out of a sense that what needed to be done is

what got done. God never hit the weekend and said, "Thank me, it's Friday."

The Spiritual Dynamics

For a long time, I didn't understand the spiritual significance of sloth. I thought it was simply a matter of developing better work habits, becoming more motivated, of working harder, or perhaps just working smarter.

A billion-dollar cottage industry — the motivational market — has emerged precisely because we no longer understand the true significance of sloth and hence don't know how to respond to it. We go from motivational speaker to seminar to book to tape, as if we were basketballs with slow leaks trying to find someone or something to pump us up, to counteract our tendency to deflate. We pay money for people to quote platitudes and cite bad social science research and tell exciting stories that psyche us up to run a little faster, work a little harder, stay a little later.

Not that motivation is bad. I'd rather be motivated than de-motivated. But isn't there something deeper?

The Bible doesn't really call us to be more motivated or more productive workers. The relevant image in Scripture is fruitfulness. Not busyness. Not even productivity. Fruitfulness.

A godly person, the Bible says, is like a tree planted by rivers of living waters. Trees are not frenzied or frantic. They do not attend seminars on "releasing the redwood within them." They do not chant slogans: "What the sap can conceive, the branch can achieve." They do not consume vast amounts of caffeine to keep up their adrenaline.

Trees are unhurried. They are full of activity, though most of it is unseen. Mostly, a tree knows where its nourishment comes from. It is deeply rooted. It does not wander from its source. It is not easily distracted. A tree has learned to abide.

"If you abide in me," Jesus says, "you will bear much fruit" (John 15:5).

Abiding in Christ is the great antithesis to sloth. Sloth demands no effort but gives no rest. Abiding is effort-filled but is the place of nourishment and renewal. "Take my yoke upon you . . ." Jesus says (a surprising offer to make to tired people) "and you will find rest for your souls" (Matt. 11:29).

One year in the middle of the Easter season, I found myself lacking the energy to minister effectively or even pray well. I talked about this with my spiritual director, and she suggested that I get up for an hour at night to reflect on the crucifixion and pray. (She had two techniques for waking up at 1:00 A.M. One was to set my alarm clock. The other — designed to let my spouse sleep undisturbed — was to drink three glasses of water before going to bed.)

I had never done anything like that before, and frankly the thought of losing sleep was not appealing. But I was amazed by the uniqueness of praying at night. There was a stillness that is never available during the day. Somehow the reality of another world was much more accessible at an hour when my usual world was so quiet and remote. In the darkness and the eerie silence, I felt as if I was actually "keeping watch" with Jesus. And in keeping watch with him, I found rest for my soul.

The irony of sloth, of course, is that it isn't even refreshing. You never talk to someone who says, "I vegged out in front of the TV last night from dinner to bedtime, from Dan Rather to David Letterman, and it was such a life-enhancing experience. Today I feel so full of vigor and energy; it's good to be alive!"

Our society teaches us to oscillate between frenzy and collapse. We commute and cocoon. We have lost the rhythm that develops between abiding and fruitfulness.

Abiding consists of all those activities of body and mind that put me in the place where I can receive life from God, including such things as prayer, sleep, solitude, eating, hobbies, and long conversations. Of course, none of these activities in and of themselves guarantee that I will be abiding. They become abiding when I learn how to meet God in them.

Giving Sloth the Second Degree

To keep sloth at bay, I have learned to ask myself four questions periodically (assuming I've made room in my schedule to do this).

1. *Has sloth shown up in my life with my family?*

For me this is sloth's first likely hiding place. Sometimes I operate under the delusion that I can get away with channeling my best time and energy to ministry and giving my family what is left over. But I get little warning signs:

A married couple sits in my office. She grew up a PK; she pours out her anguish over how her father spoke so movingly about family life and attending to feelings and right priorities, while life at home was another story. She is still trying to pick up the pieces. I struggle to keep listening. Inside I am asking myself, *Is that me? I think I'm on the right track with my kids, but how do I know? Will one of my little girls be in somebody's office in fifteen years? What will she say about her daddy?*

Though the pastoral schedule constantly hammers away at my goal, I want at least half of my best energy to go for my family.

2. *Am I spending too much time on urgent tasks?*

Stephen Covey, author of *Seven Habits of Highly Effective People*, offers a helpful distinction. He notes that work can be placed in one of four quadrants, depending on its degree of urgency and its degree of importance.

Quadrant I is work that is both urgent and important, for instance, sermon preparation: important because it's one of my critical contributions, urgent because Sunday's coming!

Quadrant II is work that is important but not urgent, for instance, developing leaders: the church will be crippled if this doesn't happen, but this task has no natural deadlines as does preaching.

Quadrant III involves tasks that feel urgent but lack importance; answering the telephone usually falls in this category.

Quadrant IV tasks are neither urgent nor important: reading the cartoons in LEADERSHIP, unless you find one you can use in the sermon.

One of the keys to effectiveness is finding which tasks lie in quadrant II, because unless I am intentional in my approach to them, they're likely to go undone. The real danger, Covey points out, is that the human machine is only wired to be able to cope with a certain amount of urgency. If I spend too much time in quadrant I, I'm likely to spend most of the rest of my time in quadrant-IV activities as a way of recovering. I become vulnerable to sloth. Once I've identified my primary quadrant-II tasks, I can realign my schedule.

This has helped me eliminate some quadrant-IV activities. I'm currently on a year-long "TV fast." It started accidentally; I decided during a time of repentance-focused praying to give up TV for a week. I found myself spending more time with my children at night, having leisurely talks with my wife, going to bed earlier and waking up more refreshed. I said to myself, "Why is this penance? This should be celebration; watching TV should be an act of penance!"

3. *Am I serving in areas where my giftedness and sense of fulfillment lie?*

I want and need to be giving a good portion of my time to tasks that use my gifts — preaching and leadership, for example. These tend to energize me, and they tend to be tasks that are in fact needful. On the other hand, counseling drains me in a hurry. Too much of that, and I find I don't have the energy or will to give myself in areas where I could really contribute to the kingdom.

You can only push this question so far, though. "That's not my area of giftedness" can easily become a cop-out for refusing a Spirit-prompted call to servanthood. I'm not sure any of the disciples would have said taking a basin and washing everybody else's dirty feet fell in their area of giftedness.

And it provides a dangerously spiritual-sounding reason for not working in the nursery: "Sorry, I took the 'Wagner-Houts Modified Spiritual Gift Inventory'; 'nursery' is not in my area of giftedness." (I keep hoping one of the more radical paraphrases of the New Testament will translate Ephesians 4:11, "And God has appointed some to be apostles, some to be prophets, some to be evangelists, and some to be nursery workers. . . ." It would become the pew Bible of choice in every church in America.)

Nonetheless, if I find myself working consistently outside of my giftedness, I need to rearrange my activities.

4. *Am I living too much in the future?*

Sometimes I get overwhelmed because I look too far ahead. In my first year of preaching regularly I was badly afflicted with PMS (pre-message syndrome). I was cranky, irritable, and suffered mood swings that became more extreme as Sunday approached. This was compounded by a crowded schedule — in addition to virtually full-time ministry I had a 25-hour-a-week internship in clinical psychology, and I had to write a dissertation. For an entire year, except for those weeks when I did not preach, I didn't take a day off.

I found something odd. The more hours I put in, the less productive I became. I would spend hours staring at a blank sheet of paper, thinking of all the sermons I would have to write that year, wondering where all the ideas would come from.

I finally realized that my busy calendar was a bad mistake. I was paralyzed from doing the few things I needed to do today by the many things I needed to do tomorrow.

Psychologist David Burns talks about how irrational this is. Imagine, he writes, that every time you sat down to eat, you thought about all the food you would have to eat during your lifetime. Imagine a huge room with tons of meat, vegetables, Twinkies and Fritos, and thousands of gallons of ice cream — and before you die you've got to consume every bite.

"Just the sight of it all makes me sick," we would say. "This one little meal is a drop in the bucket. There's no point in eating it."

The secret is, of course, we eat only one meal at a time. It's amazing how much we can consume in a lifetime if we eat it one meal at a time.

"Therefore don't worry about tomorrow, for tomorrow will worry about itself. Each day has trouble enough of its own."

Scott Peck says, "Those who are in the relatively more advanced stages of spiritual growth are the very ones most aware of their own laziness. It is the least lazy who know themselves to be sluggish. . . . The fight against entropy never ends."

I'm hardly in the advanced stages of spiritual growth, but becoming aware of my sloth has advanced my spiritual growth. I've seen sloth for what it is, even in its subtle disguises. And I've learned, as Peck notes, that life is a constant choice between comfort and growth.

As for me and my ministry, I've chosen growth. And I'll start on that tomorrow, right after I get through typing that newsletter article.

God values some things more than church unity, things like obedience, truth, and integrity.

— Richard Exley

CHAPTER FIVE

Confronting the Fear of Controversy

I clearly remember the first time my church leaders discussed our church's stance regarding pro-life involvement. A small group within our congregation had presented a proposal to the board requesting permission to begin a crisis pregnancy program.

Our discussion was intense. "I will vote in favor of the proposal," said one board member, "only if we include strict guidelines prohibiting any form of public protest against abortion."

Others expressed similar reservations. We eventually approved the group's request, but this was only the beginning of what would become one of the most controversial issues of my twelve years of ministry at Christian Chapel in Tulsa, Oklahoma.

Superheated issues in our society have a way of starting fires within the church walls. Political wars can become church wars. Of no issue is that more true than abortion.

As a pastor, I had been reticent to get involved. In the course of everyday ministry, I take enough shots without asking to be shot. I'm more interested in calming church controversy than creating it. Like most pastors, I like people to like me. The last thing I want to do is make people in my church angry.

In the end, I overcame my fears and got involved in the controversial, and I made my church angry! But I learned a lot along the way about how to handle such issues.

Be Open to God

In August 1988 as I watched a national newscast from the Democratic National Convention in Atlanta, the news anchor reported that Randall Terry and a group of anti-abortion demonstrators were using their bodies to barricade abortion clinics. They were arrested and jailed. Many refused to give their names, identifying themselves as "Baby Doe." I questioned their tactics, but I was challenged by their commitment.

After the convention ended, Operation Rescue, as it was being called, passed from the news but not from my thoughts. A recurring question haunted me: *Would I do whatever the Lord asked to end abortion on demand?*

In the ensuing weeks, my inner turmoil deepened. I didn't question whether abortion was right or wrong. Both Scripture and science had convinced me that life begins at conception: therefore abortion is morally wrong, since it's the taking of human life. In my mind the baby's right to live outweighed the mother's right to choose.

The conflict arose over my obedience, my level of commitment: How would I respond to this great tragedy?

I had serious reservations about Christians committing civil disobedience. I have a deep respect for both the law and the governing authorities, as prescribed in Romans 13. But I also knew that respect for the law doesn't mean blind allegiance. Blind compliance has historically produced human rights abuses of the most serious kind, including the Jewish Holocaust.

I was also concerned about my relationship with our denomination. Traditionally, we have distanced ourselves from anything political or social in nature. If I became involved in any serious attempt to end abortion on demand, I feared I might jeopardize my ordination, especially if I participated in civil disobedience.

Of equal concern was my relationship with Christian Chapel. I was the senior pastor. I knew how tense the board meeting had been. I anticipated far greater controversy if I myself became involved in some form of public, confrontational pro-life activity.

Less nobly, I feared arrest and imprisonment. What would happen to my wife, Brenda, if I went to jail for weeks or months? How would she support herself if my income was suddenly cut off?

To escape the torment of my conscience, I plunged into my work, initiating new programs at the church and increasing my counseling load. Nothing helped. Like the fugitive in Francis Thompson's *Hound of Heaven*, I encountered God at every turn; he wouldn't let the issue leave my consciousness.

Throughout this time of uncertainty, I did not discuss the issue with anyone in the church. I didn't want to cause any confusion until I was committed to a course of action. Finally, after nearly nine months of agonizing indecision, I still wasn't decided on what my involvement would be, but I prayed, "Lord, I will take up my cross and follow in whatever way you lead. I will even 'rescue' if that is what you want me to do."

For the first time in many months, I experienced an inner peace. The future was still uncertain; I was no less afraid, but I no longer felt as if I was fighting against God.

Time Your Moves

With my new resolve, I decided to preach an anti-abortion sermon. This wasn't my first. At Christian Chapel, we addressed this issue at least once a year, always on Sanctity of Life Sunday.

But this was different. This was Mother's Day 1989, not Sanctity of Life Sunday. Mother's Day is for mothers, the one Sunday out of the entire year when they expect to be honored. On Mother's Day, the entire family comes to church anticipating a "warm fuzzy" — a tribute extolling the virtues of motherhood.

Instead I broadsided them with a graphic message detailing the horrors of abortion, ending with a ringing challenge to act now!

Why was I so insensitive? At the time, I was convinced the Holy Spirit had directed me. Now I'm not so sure. I reasoned that Mother's Day would be a day when our women would be sensitized to the meaning of motherhood and the value of children, and therefore more outraged by the horrors of abortion.

I was right, at least about the outrage part. Several mothers, horrified by my graphic description of aborted babies, fled the sanctuary before I could finish my sermon. I learned later that many others were offended, and at least one family left the church.

Unfortunately, my timing diverted the people's focus from the tragedy of abortion to a discussion of my taste in preaching such a sermon on Mother's Day.

Keep Your Balance

But I didn't give up my desire to demonstrate our commitment to the sanctity of human life, and the congregation and I quickly found ourselves at a philosophical impasse.

Although virtually every member felt that abortion was wrong, we were clearly divided on the church's responsibility. Some argued against legislating morality, saying that free moral agents have the right to make morally wrong choices.

Others, though, argued that no one's "right" to sin gives them the right to take a life, that abortion must be outlawed to protect the innocent. That was also my position.

Still others thought our involvement should be limited to prayer. They reasoned that this was a spiritual issue that could be resolved only through intercession.

I agreed but pointed out, "Historically the church has combined prayer with some form of direct action. In missions, it's prayer and witness. In Christian service, it's prayer and acts of mercy. In fighting abortion, shouldn't we use both intercession and intervention?"

But the complaint I heard most concerned the "needs" of church attenders. Again and again church members said, "People don't come to church to hear about abortion but to have their spiritual needs met."

That complaint gave me pause. I was committed to the needs of my flock. Yet I also felt impassioned about the injustices of society. How to balance the needs of my members with prophetic action became a constant challenge, one I'm not sure I always managed well.

I easily could have become a one-issue preacher during this time. But the pastoral staff and elder board held me accountable and kept me in balance. Abortion is a great evil and one the church must address, but the message of the gospel is still "Christ and him crucified."

My insensitive Mother's Day sermon opened my eyes to the silent needs of some in my congregation. So intent to preach prophetically on the horrors of abortion, I had overlooked the pain of abortion's other victim — the mother. Many women who have made this choice struggle with guilt and regret. Apart from the grace of Jesus Christ, they have no way of escaping the painful consequences of their tragic decision.

After counseling several women who had aborted their children, I became more sensitive to their needs in my preaching. While some needed to hear the prophetic message of the gospel, others needed to receive forgiveness and healing that comes only through Christ.

Prepare for Loving Confrontation

Christian Chapel soon became known as the pro-life voice for the Christian community in Tulsa. We organized a citywide pro-life rally attended by more than 2,000 concerned citizens. Six weeks later we staged a prayer vigil in front of the local abortion clinic, attended by scores of clergy and nearly 600 pro-life believers.

On the anniversary of the Roe v. Wade decision, we held a memorial service in our church yard, attended by 1,500 people of all faiths. In 1991 I chaired the committee for the Rally for Life at the state capital, attended by more than 14,000. Repeatedly, the local television news interviewed me concerning abortion issues, and several colleges and universities invited me to speak.

Our church swung into action. Members of our congregation picketed the local abortion clinics. Others counseled on the sidewalks leading to the abortion clinics, telling the mothers who came for abortions about other alternatives. Still others opened their homes to single pregnant women, and physicians from our church provided their services at no cost to these expectant mothers.

As a result of the loving concern they experienced, many troubled women found emotional healing and committed their lives to follow Christ. Many childless couples adopted babies who, except for our intervention, would have died at the hands of abortionists.

Keep Your Priorities Clear

As I review the past four years, I see that the cost of obeying what we felt was our responsibility has been high. Although all the leaders of Christian Chapel supported my efforts, others in the congregation did not. Some of the more imaginative dissenters accused me of having a mid-life crisis. Others suggested that if the official board did not censor me, I would lead the church astray. Over a period of months, scores of people left the church.

One of my greatest temptations was to sacrifice my integrity to maintain church unity. Things were going well at the church: attendance, baptisms, and giving — all were up. Why risk rocking the boat over something as controversial as abortion?

I returned again and again to the words of Christ, "Do not suppose that I have come to bring peace to the earth. I did not come to bring peace, but a sword. For I have come to turn 'a man against his father, a daughter against her mother, a daughter-in-law against her mother-in-law — a man's enemies will be the members of his own household' " (Matt. 10:34–36).

I finally concluded that God values some things more than unity. Among them are obedience, truth, and integrity.

Stay for the Long Haul

"The race," wrote King Solomon, "is not to the swift or the battle to the strong."

Nowhere is this more evident than in pro-life work. Mobilizing a congregation to pursue any vision — especially something psychologically threatening like action against abortion — takes time. Just as it takes more than one sermon to teach stewardship or prayer, so it takes several sermons over a period of time to lead a church into a controversial issue.

I found that as our members participated in pro-life activities, their commitment increased, gradually rubbing off on others in the congregation. One of the least threatening ways we introduced our people to action was by encouraging their participation in Life Chain, a peaceful demonstration of pro-life supporters who hold signs and link arms in communities across the country the first Sunday in October. We also encouraged members to serve as volunteers in a local crisis pregnancy center.

"When you fill a swamp with stones," said missionary Frank Laubach, who pioneered literacy programs in underprivileged countries, "a hundred loads may disappear under the water before a stone appears on the surface, but all of them are necessary."

When confronting controversial issues, our prayers and efforts seem to disappear from sight, seemingly without effect. But I'm convinced that every action I take counts, and the involvement of my church makes a difference.

It is not the ministry that makes me angry. It's me that makes me angry.

— *John Ortberg*

CHAPTER SIX

Pastoral Anger: Murder in the Cathedral

Henri Nouwen has put his finger on something that for a long time I did not realize about myself:

"Anger in particular seems close to a professional vice in the contemporary ministry. Pastors are angry at their leaders for not leading and at their followers for not following. They are angry at those who do not come to church, and angry at those who do come for coming without enthusiasm.

"They are angry at their families, who make them feel guilty, and angry at themselves for not being who they want to be. This is not an open, blatant, roaring anger, but an anger hidden behind the smooth word, the smiling face, and the polite handshake. It is a frozen anger, an anger which settles into a biting resentment and slowly paralyzes a generous heart.

"If there is anything that makes the ministry look grim and dull, it is this dark, insidious anger in the servants of Christ."

I have anger in me. This realization was somewhat unexpected: I don't see myself as an angry person. I have always thought of myself as a peacemaker by nature. I don't explode. I have never been a screamer. I'm a Baptist, but emotionally I'm really more of a Presbyterian.

And yet I have anger in me. I know this because it surfaces when I don't expect it.

I remember a hurtful thing a deacon said to me a long time ago. Years have passed; surely I'm too big to be bothered by such a little thing, yet there it is. The scene gets replayed in my mind, only with alternate endings. I find myself fantasizing about how to get even, how to hurt back. Where does this come from?

I'm driving home after a long and pressured day of ministry. I inadvertently cut someone off; he catches up and honks and gestures. Suddenly I find myself trembling with rage; I want to cut him off again; I want to hurt him. Where does this come from?

Learning from my anger and acquiring the skill to manage it well have become lifelong goals of mine. I have found a number of questions that help me achieve them.

What Is Anger?

Whole forests have been cut down to provide paper for the books that seek to answer this question. I think the best answer is that anger is physiological arousal — heart-racing, adrenaline-pumping, blood-pressure raising arousal — along with my own hostile or indignant interpretation of what caused the arousal.

One of the most common anger problems among pastors is to deny or misread our experiences of anger, which also guarantees we will express it in destructive ways.

Let's say there is a part of my job that I should be doing more effectively, a part I've simply been neglecting. A member of the ministry team tells me this, appropriately, graciously, but quite candidly.

I know that he is right, yet I feel hurt. This tears at the myth of my ability to be a "super pastor," makes me feel quite ordinary and somewhat embarrassed. His observation is obvious enough that I cannot deny it, but my response is not healthy either. For the remainder of our conversation, I go into withdrawal. I am polite and make no direct complaints. Without thinking about it, I avoid direct eye contact and physical touch and do not smile genuinely; my tone of voice says, "Stay away."

After you've known somebody long enough, you learn how to gauge this withdrawal precisely: clear enough so that the other person unmistakably feels it; subtle enough so that if he asks, "Have you got a problem?" I can respond, "No. Why do you ask? You got a problem?"

For I am Scandinavian, and we don't get mad. Hurt, sure. Offended, often. Wounded so that we can never recover and never forget — you bet. But not mad.

What Makes Pastors Angry?

The earliest discussion I can remember having with my parents about church was when I asked them, "Why is the pastor always mad at us?"

As I've grown older and wiser and learned the subtleties of human behavior, I've realized my naive childhood perceptions were right on target. There's something about pastoral ministry that produces (or attracts) angry people. Why?

Is it because we serve an angry God, as in Jonathan Edwards's famous sermon, "Sinners in the hands of an angry God"? Okay, at least God's anger can be trusted; it is just another facet of his love — "Anger is the fluid that love bleeds when you cut it," C. S. Lewis wrote. But sinners in the hands of angry pastors? That's another story. That's murder in the cathedral.

One reason we're angry is because we are constantly being

reviewed. Pastoring is a strange job. We are called to shepherd sheep. But the sheep in our charge are also our bosses. And sometimes they act like it.

Perhaps the most obvious and vulnerable area in which we're reviewed is preaching. It's helpful to be (tactfully) critiqued. And it is right for pastors to want to do well. But it is painfully tempting to allow Sunday morning to become a kind of spiritual performance on which my emotional well-being hinges. When I succumb, I feel trapped, and trapped ministers are angry ministers.

Sometimes the negative reviews are relatively easy to dismiss. At one church, an attender regularly informed my wife if I failed to button my coat while preaching. (As a passive-aggressive response, I considered preaching without buttoning my shirt.)

Other critiques dig deeper: "I'm not being fed." For most pastors, this is tantamount to waving a red flag in front of a wounded bull. The not-so-subtle message is "You're just tickling people's ears."

In addition, vision, leadership, interpersonal skills, the general state of the church — all of these are fair game for the congregation's evaluation — and dry tinder that sparks into pastoral anger.

Thomas Merton wrote somewhere that the false self is fabricated by social compulsions. "Compulsive ministry" is the kind of ministry that produces angry and resentful ministers. Compulsive ministry is when I base my worth on satisfying the standards that define success in my little world. Budgets must be met, attendance must be raised, people must be happy, programs must thrive. Compulsive ministry is in the deepest sense being "conformed to the world."

I recognize my compulsivity when someone says, "Why don't we have a . . . (fill in the blank: singles ministry, stronger missions program, social awareness committee, American flag in the sanctuary, greater commitment to our community, old-fashioned revival with a traveling evangelist and good accordion music)." I don't think I ever hear that without feeling a twinge of guilt. This sets me up for resentment: *Why don't they do it themselves? Why do I have to keep everybody pumped up?* In my compulsivity, I feel like a circus performer who keeps plates spinning on top of sticks; if I ever stop, they'll all come crashing down.

This pattern of behavior leads me to another insight: it is not the ministry that makes me angry; it's me that makes me angry.

Because anger is such a powerful emotion, it feels as if it is being caused by something "out there." My experience tells me that it's rude drivers and surly deacons. Instead, I have to admit that it is not events but my interpretation of events that makes me angry.

It is nine o'clock at night. My four-year-old gets out of bed and cautiously, tentatively comes down the stairs, in violation of curfew. However, I have nothing to do, nowhere to go; I am relaxed and at peace with the world. *Look at the little tyke,* I think. *Only a few more years to enjoy Kodak moments like this, and then he'll be grown. How brave and adventurous he is, risking punishment to explore the unknown world of the night. He's just like his father.*

Another night, same hour, same child, same father. But this time I have reached the end of a long and stressful day, and I have to finish a chapter on anger before I go to bed. The little tyke walks down the stairs, but my mind plays a different tune: *Only a few precious moments to get my work done, and Eddie Munster here can't stay in bed. Sure, sneak down the stairs, kid. Go ahead, make my day. The question you've got to ask yourself is, "Do I feel lucky?" How rebellious and disobedient he is, defying parental authority ordained by God because of his relativistic narcissism. He's just like his mother!*

Notice that the external event was identical in both situations. But one time it led to joy, the other time, to anger. The critical variable was my interpretation of what was happening. This is universally true. It is not what other people say or do but the way I think about it that gives rise to anger.

Lots of people have the power to hurt or frustrate me. Only one has the power to make me angry. Me.

If it is true that no one else can make me angry, it is even more true that no one else can make me respond aggressively or inappropriately when I feel anger. It often seems that way because my response to feeling anger has become so routine that it seems "automatic." It feels as if the person or event triggered my anger and *caused* my response.

The truth is my response is learned behavior. I learned it long ago, from people I grew up around, learned it so informally that I was not aware that I was learning anything.

Tommy Bolt has been described as the angriest golfer in the history of a game that has stimulated the secretion of more bile than any other single human activity outside of war and denominational meetings. One (possibly apocryphal) story recalls a time he was giving a group lesson on how to hit a ball out of a sand trap. He called his 11-year-old son over.

"Show the people what you've learned from your father to do when your shot lands in the sand," he said. The boy picked up a wedge and threw it as high and as far as he could.

The good news is what can be learned can be unlearned. It is possible for me to manage my anger in a God-honoring way: to "be angry and sin not."

How Do I Handle Anger?

Anger is an inescapable fact of life. But the *experience* of anger is different from the *expression* of anger. What I do with that anger, how I express and manage it, is another matter.

It's helpful to identify how I usually express my anger. In *Make Anger Your Ally*, Neil Warren outlines four common profiles of anger management, which I have adapted for pastors.

The first might be termed *pastors who blow up*. You never have to wonder when these people are angry. They have a little sign on their desk that reads, I DON'T GET ULCERS, I GIVE THEM. Their sermons are illustrated with stories of General Patton, Woody Hayes, Zsa Zsa Gabor, Mount Saint Helens. Peter Cartwright, the nineteenth-century circuit-riding preacher who bodily threw out inattentive or distracting attenders, who publicly said to a deacon, "Brother, one more prayer like that, and hell will freeze over," would fit in this category.

The second group is *pastors who burn up* — who somaticize their anger. These people hold it in, conceal what they feel. They are often unaware of being angry, but inside it eats at them the way acid corrodes a battery.

They may not recognize their anger, but they can't escape its effects. One author identified over fifty illnesses affected by unprocessed anger. Pastors who burn up are often found on the prayer chain, victims of one sickness or another. Because of their non-confrontive style, they often find themselves surrounded by openly aggressive types (like the pastor lying in the hospital who received a note from the board, "Dear Pastor, the board voted to wish you a speedy recovery, seven to five with two abstentions").

The third type are *pastors who pout*. They retaliate though not aggressively; they prefer to inflict guilt by suffering unfairly. Pastoral ministry is especially attractive to these ministers because it offers such rich opportunity for martyrdom, yet without the nuisance of actually having to die.

The Bible is full of them: Jonah, calling for Dr. Kevorkian because Nineveh was spared and a worm had eaten his shade-vine. The prodigal son's elder brother: "Sure, Dad, you go have a party. I'll just stay out here and work the fields just as I have my whole life without anyone even saying thank you. Don't worry about me."

Of the four, this is probably my tendency. I pout pretty well. Number one sounds like more fun, but I'm a pastor. I do number one in my heart, but on the outside I do number three.

The fourth group consists of *pastors who catch up*. These are the sneaky ones. They'll jab and needle and dig with words funny enough to get away with but designed to do damage. Elders get frustrated with them because these pastors "forget" to return phone calls, or they show up late for appointments. They are masters of (often unconscious) sabotage.

At least with the first group, you know where you stand. With this group, after one of their zingers, you ask, "Where is all this blood coming from?" And then you look down and realize it's coming from you. If you call them on it, will they admit they're acting out of anger? Noooooo — the gutless little wimps. Of all anger styles, this is the most infuriating. They make me so angry, I could pout.

How Do I Manage Anger with My Children?

Maybe the most accurate gauge to read on how and why I manage — or mismanage — anger is to examine how my anger comes out with my children. For with them, my anger has few external constraints. They can't yell back. They can't get offended, withdraw their pledges, and start attending other families. So I can see what my anger will do unimpeded.

We went to Kinderphoto to have a family photo taken for the holidays. I don't know who invented the idea of little kids getting dressed up, sitting still, and smiling for some stranger behind a huge camera. This was a nightmare. We put our kids on the giant rocking horse, and our youngest daughter was terrified. She sobbed uncontrollably. We made funny faces, bribed her with sugar cookies — to no avail.

So I got mad and threatened to spank her, not an effective way to get a smile from a two year old. Soon her sister was crying; the photographer was crying; other families were waiting to take their turn, and their kids were crying. They began to chant 1 Timothy 3:5, "If anyone does not know how to manage his own family, how can he take care of God's church?"

So I pulled our youngest child off the horse and said to her gently, "Do you wish you had Baby Tweezers right now?" Baby Tweezers was her favorite doll.

With big tears in her eyes, my daughter answered, "Yes."

"Well," I continued, "if you ever want to see Baby Tweezers alive again, I better see your face radiate with mirth until that big man behind the camera says we're done."

Only later did I realize what was going on. My concern was not for the picture. I needed to look as if I was in control. I was more concerned with my need to look like a good parent, to convince people I was the right kind of father, than I was about the well-being of my children. And if they don't turn on the obedience to create that appearance, I'll take my anger out on them.

I don't want to be that kind of father. I want to be a memory-making, life-affirming, magic-moment-creating kind of daddy.

Sometimes I convince myself that I am. But moments like this show how hurry sickness and self-absorption block that goal and fuel so much of my anger, at home and at church.

Do I Enjoy Being Angry?

I must enjoy anger because I work so hard to keep it alive. A grudge is like a baby; it has to be nursed if it's going to survive. Anger is inevitable. Resentment is optional.

Frederick Buechner writes, "Of the Seven Deadly Sins, anger is possibly the most fun. To lick your wounds, to smack your lips over grievances long past, to roll your tongue over the prospect of bitter confrontations still to come, to savor to the last toothsome morsel both the pain you are given and the pain you are giving back — in many ways it is a feast fit for a king. The chief drawback is that what you are wolfing down is yourself. The skeleton at the feast is you."

I need to be careful about preaching out of anger, precisely because it can be fun. Once I was preaching about the prodigal son's elder brother, and my eyes landed on a man who was legalistic and who resisted change in the church. Suddenly I was filled with righteous indignation. I didn't stare at him — no one there could have known about this — but in my heart I was saying to him, "This is you. The elder brother is you." This made my delivery pretty passionate — probably helped the sermon out. But for me it was a spiritually destructive practice. It's a form of pulpit abuse.

Certainly at times preaching will be done with anger. The words of the prophets were often spoken directly out of their anger. If Martin Luther King, Jr., hadn't given voice to prophetic anger, our society would be immeasurably poorer. But he always taught that words of judgment must be filtered through love before they can be safely pronounced: "We must meet the forces of hate with the power of love; we must meet physical force with soul force."

How Do Healthy Pastors Manage Anger?

How can pastors, who are supposed to model patience and love, express anger appropriately in the church setting (meaning, without losing their credibility, jobs, or sanity)?

Three strategies help me: (1) clarify what it is I really want (and value) when I'm angry, (2) create a strategy that is more likely to achieve it, and (3) find a trustworthy person *outside* the church to whom I can freely, fully express my anger.

I once heard from a third party that a former deacon had criticized the church and me. My first impulse was to criticize the former deacon, by way of defending my reputation and harming his.

Ventilation for ventilation's sake may feel good at the moment, but it almost never brings about what I really want. If I can identify what I clearly want (as opposed to a reflexive desire to hurt), I can choose a strategy that will help me get there.

I recognized what I really wanted was a church where this kind of communication did not go on. I wanted to be the kind of person who could confront this honestly and in love. So I called the former deacon to arrange an appointment.

At this point, it got more complicated. He said (I know this sounds hard to believe) he refused to meet with me until I changed the church motto.

The motto printed on church stationary seemed to me fairly innocuous: "Reaching up and reaching out." I found myself getting angrier. *This is so stupid!* The only just solution entailed having him shot, and this didn't seem practical at the time. So I called on another resource I think is indispensable for pastors: a person outside the church with whom I can talk openly about all details of my life.

Pastors need an outside "ventilatee" because there are aspects of our church-directed anger that are unfair to burden any church member with.

After I had dumped the whole load of my frustration and hurt with my friend, we were able to devise a plan together that would best lead toward reconciliation.

Effective anger management, then, has become a lifetime goal for me. Because if I don't become the kind of husband and father and pastor that I dream of being, that will make me really angry. And eternity is a long time to pout.

Mike would discover that in order to overcome despair, he would have to be willing to let go of the things he so feared losing.

— Mark Galli

CHAPTER SEVEN
When You Can't Hold On

Michael Wells stood in the kitchen looking at his wife, Joanne, who had just said she needed to talk. Her eyes — sad, fearful, almost panicky — were filled with tears. She started shaking and blurted out, "I don't think you realize how unhappy I am!"

Mike's body turned cold. "What do you mean?"

"I'm thinking about moving out."

The words echoed off the dull tile counters. A heaviness settled on Mike, and his mind went numb. As a Methodist pastor, he had heard parishioners tell him what he thought were clichéd reactions to shocking news. Now they weren't clichés: *This is not happening to me*, he thought. *I'll wake up any minute, and it will be a horrible dream.*

"Why didn't you tell me? I didn't know you were unhappy."

Joanne had been seeing a therapist for a year. Mike had asked her what she talked about in her sessions, but she had always answered vaguely: "Oh, about my parents." Mike had learned that with Joanne the more you push, the more stubborn she became. So he hadn't pursued it.

"This is not fair!" he now continued. "We should go to therapy together before you move out."

Through her tears, Joanne just kept repeating, "I'm just so unhappy. I need time alone." She promised to be gone only three months.

The next few May Saturdays, Joanne went apartment hunting in Austin, Texas, where they lived, and within a month she was ready. The June weekend she planned to move, Mike had previously planned a choir trip for his youth group. That Friday, he and Joanne went to breakfast at a little bakery. Over the aroma of croissants and coffee, they chatted nervously about this and that, and then it came time to go to work. Matter of factly, with promises to keep in close contact, they got into their separate cars and drove their separate ways.

Mike, before turning toward the church, stopped and watched Joanne drive away. "Good-bye, Joanne," he muttered. He wondered if she would ever come back.

Two days later, Mike was exhausted when he returned home and depressed when he walked inside. He flicked on the lights; half of their belongings were gone; it looked so lonely. He tried to sleep but spent most the night crying silently.

That summer, always blistering in Austin, Mike lived in a cold daze. Though Joanne said she would return in three months, Mike feared she wouldn't. As a minister, he was ashamed, and he believed his very calling was threatened, so he told only one or two close friends at the church. Sometimes Mike would weep. Sometimes his shoulders and arms would quiver, as if he wanted to hit somebody. Mostly he felt like giving up.

One morning as he stepped into the shower, Mike noticed a black spider on the shower wall. He squirted it with water and knocked it to the stall floor. The water pushed it toward the drain, but the spider tenaciously held on, giving way only slowly. Gallons of water poured over it, but the spider hugged the floor. A minute passed before the spider was finally swallowed by the drain.

That's when Mike fell apart. He burst into tears and sobbed, as he hadn't sobbed in years. *I'm going crazy*, he thought, *I've totally lost it. I'm out of control.* He knew he was that little spider. He had been holding on against tremendous odds, holding on to his dreams, to his life, but he realized it wasn't enough. Everything he had lived for was about to wash down the drain.

During the next three years, Mike would time and again wrestle despair. He would discover that in order to overcome this enemy, he would have to lose the very things he despaired of losing: his marriage, his ministry, and his faith. And today, he thanks God for it.

Soured Dream

The first to go was the marriage, the hinge of Mike's life.

A couple of years before Joanne moved out, Mike had happily told people he felt "very married." They had been together about eight years by then and had just bought a home in suburban Austin. Mike was associate pastor of Aldersgate Methodist, and Joanne worked in personnel at a company that made computer disk drives. And most important, Joanne had finally agreed to have children, even though she feared the surgery it would require.

For Mike, everything was falling into place. Though he'd had many dreams about his career, it was visions of family that most captivated his imagination. A house in the lawn-lined suburbs, a wife, children, a dog — that was life. Joanne's willingness to get pregnant was the finishing touch.

The year they tried to get Joanne pregnant was one of delighted anticipation. They talked about the baby's room, whether it should be painted blue or rose, where the crib would go. When Joanne bought a colorful mobile or a furry stuffed animal, they would ooh and aah.

And it was a time of making love, the special kind of love a man and a woman share when they are trying to create new life.

Then slowly, almost imperceptively to Mike, things started deteriorating. Joanne became increasingly critical. Mike was too heavy. He wasn't in touch with his feelings. He wasn't home enough. He didn't pick up after himself.

Mike recognized these faults, and he set about to correct them. He had swelled to 300 pounds, but a diet dropped 100 pounds in a year. He went to therapy, as Joanne had been doing, and tried to better understand his feelings. He skipped some church meetings and rescheduled others so he could be home four or five nights a week. He tried to be more neat around the house.

Mike, of course, had his complaints too. Joanne was beginning to balk about having children. They made love less and less. It got to the point where Joanne didn't even want to touch Mike; she seemed repulsed by him. Oddly, the more evenings Mike spent at home, the more Joanne needed to work late.

Mike also wanted Joanne to be more open with him, to tell him what was bothering her, but when he asked, she would just clam up. He wanted her to be more willing to admit her own faults: she could give him a seventeen-point litany of his faults, but whenever he would mention merely one fault of hers, she would throw a tantrum.

Between Mike's sarcasm and Joanne's reticence, communication broke down.

Joanne would say she didn't want to talk, that she needed to get in touch with her feelings. Mike would retort in Obi-wan Kenobi fashion, "Luke, go with your feelings."

"I don't appreciate your making fun of my beliefs," she would say.

"Well, I don't appreciate hiding your feelings from me. You use this 'I don't know what I'm feeling' as an excuse not to talk to me!"

Still, Mike didn't think their problems were extraordinary, nothing other couples didn't face. Then came Joanne's announcement and move.

Dreams for a Quarter

After Joanne left, Mike grieved hard.

He slept on Joanne's side of the bed. Sometimes he would walk into her closet and just stand there, inhaling her scent, which still lingered there.

Joanne had always folded laundry on Sunday night while she watched *Murder, She Wrote*. Mike never had much interest in the show, but now on Sunday nights, he did the laundry while watching *Murder, She Wrote*.

Sometimes he would just amble around the house; it made him feel as if Joanne were still there.

One windy day in the fall, he was digging in his garden. As he planted bulbs, his tears wetted the dark, clay soil; he prayed, "God, I'm burying these dead things; someday they will be raised up into beauty and glory. I hope that someday you will raise up my marriage. You're the God of the Resurrection. Please, raise up my marriage!"

After three months were up, Joanne hesitated about coming back. They argued about it in front of their therapist for months before Joanne agreed to give it another try. Mike was ecstatic. *It's going to be all right. We're going to work it out. She's my wife again. We'll have kids together.*

The night Joanne returned, when they went to bed, Joanne rolled over to go to sleep. Mike reached over to rub her back.

Joanne bolted upright. "I can't stand it!"

"What?"

"The tension is so thick! Don't you feel it?"

"Feel what?"

Over the next few months, the marriage continued to unravel. Mike discovered some letters and other papers that suggested Joanne had been having affairs, but she explained all the evidence away. Mike agreed to believe her, but he remained suspicious and hurt.

And despairing. One Sunday night, he sat in his office holding a tiny Guatemalan worry doll. A girl in his youth group had given it to him some months before, telling him kiddingly that whenever he worried, he should rub the doll. For two hours, Mike cried in his office, praying, worrying, rubbing the little doll.

As these things go, periods of hope mixed with periods of despair. At one point, Mike was confident the marriage would last, so he agreed to take a new church in San Antonio, some eighty miles away. Joanne said she would quit her job and work on her M.B.A. Mike would move over while Joanne sold the house. Then Joanne would join him.

To prepare for the move, they held a yard sale, and one of Joanne's friends, Roger, came over to help. They were putting things on the tables when Joanne and Roger came across a box of baby things — mobiles, crib sheets, stuffed animals. They put them on the sale table.

You're going to sell that? Mike thought.

Later in the morning, a woman came up, glanced at the baby things, and asked, "How much?"

"A quarter a piece," Roger said.

"I'll take them," the woman replied.

Mike noticed that Joanne didn't even flinch. But he thought, *That's all my dreams are worth. All my dreams are being sold for twenty-five cents.* Then voices shouted from within, "You're useless. You're worse than useless!" He wanted to run around the corner of the house and cry.

When the house sold, Joanne said, "I'll move over in about a month. Let me just tie up some loose ends here." Another month turned into four, then into eight. On his days off, Mike commuted back to see Joanne and to attend counseling with her. He kept pursuing her, begging her to move. He was lonely, and a permanent separation terrified him.

But Joanne continued to waffle. At counseling she would mention how unfulfilled she felt, how unhappy she was with Mike. The next fall, by now a full two years after she first moved out, she cried to Mike, "I just can't see being married to you for the rest of my life. I just can't."

Something clicked in Mike. Pursuing her any longer was pointless. He knew now he could release his wife, his dream. Somehow things would be okay.

"You're free to go if you want," he said. "If you don't want to be married to me, you don't have to be." Mike was sad yet relieved.

He still didn't know, though, that there was more to lose.

A Way of Escape

When Joanne first moved out, Mike believed his ministry was doomed. He often hoped and prayed and dreamed of Joanne's return, but he feared she never would, and his separation was a huge contradiction for him: how could he manage a church if he couldn't manage his own marriage? He was sure he would have to give up ministry.

But to give up ministry — the thought flooded him with despair. All he'd ever done was prepare for ministry or minister. He loved to search out God's Word and then preach it to others. He was honored that in counseling people trusted him with their souls. It was a privilege to stand with people at the critical moments of their lives, at birth, marriage, and death. Ministry was, he believed, the highest calling. But it required a virtuous character, a model lifestyle — things he felt he no longer had.

His first instinct when Joanne first left, then, was to keep it a secret. He was ashamed, and he didn't want the church to know. The Sunday she left, Joanne stood up during the sharing of prayer concerns and said nothing more than, "I'm not going to be coming to church for a few weeks. I have some things to work out."

When Mike received dinner invitations for Joanne and him, he made excuses. When people asked awkward questions — "How are things going? I haven't seen Joanne for a while. Has she been going to the later service?" — Mike remained vague. He knew his excuses were paper thin, and he feared that any minute the truth would come bursting through. He was constantly nervous.

Mike even quit seeing his Christian therapist and sought someone "outside the household of faith." He figured a non-Christian counselor wouldn't be disappointed in him.

He did confide in the senior pastor and in one of the church's leaders, and the church secretary found out soon enough when Joanne put in a change of address to receive the church newsletter. Other than that, the separation remained a secret.

To resolve this great contradiction, Mike began looking for a way out of ministry. And a path, divinely ordained it seemed, appeared to open. At a gym one afternoon, Mike met Al Williams. Al invited Mike to lunch. "I'd like to talk to you about something you might find interesting," he said. Mike was lonely and intrigued, so he went.

At lunch, Al asked Mike, "How are you doing financially?"

On his associate pastor's salary, Mike was trying to pay all his usual bills plus his own therapy and for half of his and Joanne's joint counseling. "Not well," he replied.

"Well, how would you like to double your income in two years?"

Al took a napkin out and sketched a pyramid-shaped graph. "The principle of my business is this," Al said. "You work, but then you get others to work for you. It takes a lot of work and good people skills, which I see you've got, Mike. But in five years, you can be independently wealthy. You can stop working. You'll be earning close to $500,000 a year."

Mike felt a rush. One of Joanne's complaints was that as a pastor, Mike didn't earn enough. "Look at the people around us," she would gripe. "People our age have nicer cars; they have bigger homes. Some of my friends at work have private planes." Maybe he could woo Joanne back by becoming rich. He'd buy her a big house and a new car. He'd have to give up ministry, but at least he'd have his wife back, and maybe they could get back to making a family. Maybe he could at least partly live his suburban dream.

Another part of him, though, feared she would never return, in which case, his ministerial career was over. It didn't matter then. *If I'm going to be unhappy for the rest of my life, I might as well be unhappy and rich*, he thought. In either case, this business opportunity seemed a golden opportunity. Still, he had reservations, but he agreed to think about it.

The next time they met, Al brought a friend who had formerly been a minister. This former pastor gave Mike a pitch: "I used to be a pastor. But now that I make lots of money, I do even more for the kingdom of God. I could build a whole church if I wanted to." He explained to Mike how he had made over a million dollars the previous year, and how he had given $300,000 to his church. "What could your church do with that?"

At the time, Mike's church was in the middle of a building program. *If I could give my church $300,000, we could retire our debt and get that new building and beautiful new sanctuary!*

Pastoring a Therapist

Mike was all but ready to sign on when he was startled by something that happened in sessions with his therapist. At the end of one session, she asked him, "Do you have some time?"

Mike wondered what she could possibly want. "My husband just became a born-again Christian," she continued, "and I don't understand what's going on with him."

Mike grimaced inwardly and shifted in his chair. He didn't want to be a minister just then. He was getting ready to shed that role, and here this woman was seeking spiritual advice from him. But common courtesy demanded he listen.

She told him about the circumstances leading up to her husband's conversion, and how he and his minister were now witnessing to her. "I don't know what to do," she said. "They keep saying I have to give my life to Christ and surrender to his Lordship. But I keep thinking, *What if he tells me to go be a waitress?* I don't want to do that! I want to be a therapist. I want to live my own life."

Though Mike suspected it was wrong for a counselor to seek advice from the client, his pastoral self was hooked. For the next few sessions, they ended his therapy with some pastoral counseling. Soon the therapist was going to church with her husband.

As this went on, Mike began to feel God saying to him, "I still want you to be a pastor." When this thought first came up, it startled him. It had never occurred to Mike that he was still fit for ministry. At best, he would have to take a sabbatical until he got his marriage straightened out. But the more he talked with the therapist, the more she grew in faith. God was still using Mike.

And with that, Mike phoned Al Williams and gracefully declined the business offer. By the time Mike decided to stop seeing his therapist, she was attending church regularly and relishing the sermons. When they parted, she gave Mike a big hug and said, "Another client of mine is a priest. Both of you came to me within the same week. Do you think maybe God brought you guys to me?"

Mike had given up on ministry but had been given it back. But it would take one more incident before he was to have it back on the right terms.

Losing His Reputation

When Joanne began divorce proceedings, Mike had been at his new church only about a year and a half. He had spent that time building trust. In addition to the usual pastoral concern of living what he preached, Mike was anxious to move his theologically liberal congregation to a more personal, biblical faith.

Now, he figured, his year and a half of trust building was about to crumble. He had to tell the congregation of his impending divorce, and the thought filled him with dread and shame. One night, a few days before he would make the announcement, he sat despondent in his office. He was filled with grief and guilt. *I've been preaching this gospel of power and transformation, and I wasn't able to transform my marriage. What a hypocrite!*

"God, there are a lot of kids in this church," he prayed, "and they're going to grow up and remember that their minister got divorced. What's going to happen to their faith in you?"

He agonized for two hours. "How can you allow this to happen, Lord? It will hurt your reputation."

Suddenly, he had a physical sensation of God putting a hand, big and warm, on his shoulder. All the tension went out of Mike's body, and he slumped in relief. He sensed God saying, "Don't worry. I love you, and I'm with you. Just let go of the worry."

Then he was surprised by what he heard next: "You just worry about your own reputation; I'll worry about mine." Mike, a little embarrassed, thought, *Of course.* He had for years assumed that the gospel's reputation rose and fell with him; if he looked bad, so would God. He now realized there was no way out of his mess, that God would have to take care of himself. And it occurred to him that God probably very well could.

The next Sunday, Mike had an opportunity to test this new insight. As the last hymn of the worship service was being sung, Mike took off his robe; he didn't want it to be fouled by what he was about to tell his people.

"Could you please sit down," he said when the hymn finished. A few people looked quizzical. When they had settled in, Mike continued. "After years of trying, it's not working out with Joanne and me. We're going to get a divorce." He said it with composure, but inside he was sick. He talked for a minute or so and then dismissed the congregation.

He had assumed the response would be, at best, mixed. Some people just wouldn't care; they didn't know him that well. Some, though, would be offended and leave the church, maybe up to a third of the congregation, he calculated. Some of those, he was sure, would hear his announcement as an excuse to give up on God.

Afterwards, however, literally everyone in church came up and gave Mike a hug. They said they were sorry. They said they were going to be supportive. In the ensuing weeks, he discovered they were. No one left the church. No one, to this day, has criticized him for his divorce. No one's faith in God seemed disturbed.

To the contrary, and to Mike's amazement, their interest in things Christian began to flourish in some ways. People were more attentive to his preaching; they believed him when he said he was a fellow struggler seeking God's grace. And many of those divorced and widowed sought him out now because they felt he would understand their loneliness and pain.

Mike's new ministry, however, is another story. The main story here was that he had fully given up his old ministry, the one that rested on his goodness, on his reputation. He had begun to let

God be God of his ministry.

Before he could finally defeat despair, however, he had to lose one more thing: his life-long faith.

Failed Faith

When Joanne left that first summer, Mike, as he walked aimlessly around his empty house, kept hearing a voice rattling in his head: "People who love you give you away."

He tried drowning it out; he left the TV on in the bedroom and in the living room, and sometimes he turned the radio on as well. Still he heard, "People who love you give you away."

He tried exorcizing it. "God, this must be a demon. It's horrible. Take it away, now!" But it continued, "People who love you give you away." At times, he thought he was going crazy.

When nothing else worked, he decided, with the help of a therapist, to discover the source of this strange oracle. In part, it came from his childhood. Two incidents, he discovered, had long clung like a leech to his subconscious and to his faith.

At age two, Mike had contracted pneumonia and had to be hospitalized. The hospital was in Dallas, some thirty miles north of his home. It was awkward for his parents to visit, though: they had only one car, which his dad used to drive to work; his mother didn't drive. So for the two weeks he was hospitalized, his parents never visited him. Mike remembers being a scared, little two year old, absolutely alone in a strange place. He believed he had been given away.

He also remembered some incidents with his dad when he felt he had been emotionally given away. *Terror*, Mike says, is a soft word to describe how monstrous his dad could be when he got angry.

To take one example: Mike was 15 years old, and he and his dad were working on the car. Mike hated it when his dad asked him to help. His father was a handyman — and a perfectionist. Mike was a klutz. Mike was sure to blow it, and his dad was sure to blow up.

They were changing the oil in the car. His dad was under the car getting impatient trying to loosen a bolt. He yelled to Mike, "Give me the g--d--- seven-sixteenths!"

Immediately, Mike tensed. He frantically rummaged through the tool box, picking up and dropping a dozen wrenches. The more he fumbled, the angrier his father became: "G--d--- it. What's taking you so long?" Everything became a blur; Mike could hardly read the wrench sizes. In a panic, he handed one to his father.

His father rolled out from under the car and threw the wrench on the ground and swore again. "This is a nine-sixteenths. You can't even give me a g--d---- seven-sixteenths wrench." Mike remembers his dad's voice echoing off the houses down the street.

His father stood and hulked over Mike. "You are useless. You are worse than useless! I can't even count on you to help me to change the g--d--- oil!"

Mike remembers feeling as if all the neighbors stopped mowing their lawns, playing catch, doing hoola-hoops; they were all watching him as his dad screamed, "You are useless. You are worse than useless. Get out of here!" An emotionally-whipped Mike retreated to the house.

Mike learned early on to avoid experiences like that. He learned to be funny, to tell jokes, to act the clown. When he kept his dad laughing, he learned, he didn't get mad.

Most of all, he learned to be the good boy, to never make the same mistake twice, so he would never be emotionally given away. One day he was scolded by his dad for leaving his bike on the lawn. Mike never, the rest of his childhood, left his bike on the lawn.

Mike learned that when his dad was in a bad mood, he better not be idly watching TV or listening to the radio. When he heard his dad slam the car door a certain way, Mike would shut off the TV and open his homework before his dad walked in the door.

This fearful pharisaism was carried into his adult years and, in a modified form, into his relationship with God. God was more fair than his father, but he was a vending-machine God. You put a quarter in, you get the product out. He and God had this deal (though he never would have admitted it so bluntly): Mike would be a good boy, a good pastor, a good husband, a good man of God. In return, God would bless Mike with a happy family and a successful pastoral career. No one would abandon him. No one would think him useless.

Mike didn't fool himself. He didn't believe he was worth others' loyalty: his family didn't even think he was worth visiting in the hospital. He wasn't very useful: he couldn't even find "the g--d--- seven-sixteenths." But if he kept people laughing, he might fool them into thinking he was a great guy. And if he would keep his part of the bargain, God would make sure no one abandoned him.

Well, it didn't work. He had been a good husband. His wife said, "Be home." He was home. His wife said, "Lose weight." He lost weight. His wife said, "Go to counseling." He went to counseling. He had prayed about being a good husband. He had studied other marriages to improve his own. Furthermore, he was a faithful pastor and, as much as one could reasonably expect, a model of Christian behavior to his people.

But his marriage still fell apart, and with his marriage, his dreams. For months, Mike grew increasingly discouraged; though he continued in ministry, and though ministry flourished, he wasn't sure what to believe about God.

Cursing God

Slowly, and this was some months after he announced his divorce to his congregation, Mike began to realize that at the root of discouragement with his faith lay anger, anger towards God. But for a long time, he couldn't admit it. Good boys don't get angry with God; that is blasphemy.

His therapist (he was now seeing a Christian therapist) tried to explain, "Sometimes anger is a way of loving someone. It's honest. It's revealing some of your deepest emotions to another."

Mike was incredulous: "What are you talking about?" Mike had been constantly praying for God to take away his anger. He didn't want to feel anger, ever; it felt awful. Besides, God wouldn't love him if he was angry.

But the anger wouldn't dissipate. Instead it became hotter, and the pain finally became too much to bear. He decided, finally, with the encouragement of his therapist, to be honest with God; the simple fact was that God knew he was angry. If God was going to love him, he was going to have to love him with all his rage.

So he began praying, "God, I feel you failed me. I feel you're no good. For years I've been telling congregation after congregation to love and trust you. But for what? It's all been a lie and a sham. You let me down!"

His emotions fluctuated wildly for months. There were days when he basked in God's grace and mercy, and there were days when he would rage at God.

The more he raged, the more he realized the subtleties of his deal with God. He told his therapist once, "I've been trying to make God happy by giving him the one thing he wants most: souls, people to love him. And I've been giving him people for dozens of years. And he was supposed to give me something back. He failed me!"

The more he raged, the more intense became his prayers: "I wish you would reincarnate so I could kick you in the stomach! You let me down, you sob!" Mike would deliberately go out of the way to be blasphemous, cursing God in the most vile language, as if he were provoking God, testing God.

And the more he raged, amazingly, the more he experienced God. "I was shocked," he now says, "I didn't understand it. Even though I was vomiting up all this anger, God was a silent presence to me. He was more present than he had ever been. I can't explain it, but I experienced him inwardly. It was as if God, like a compassionate parent, was letting me throw a tantrum, but he wasn't going to leave me. For months, I had an on-going theophany. God was as close as breath."

One time in prayer, Mike envisioned Jesus on the cross, and he took all his blasphemous anger and poured it on him, stabbing Jesus with it, crucifying him afresh. "Christ just stayed there," he says, "letting me get all this poison out, taking it upon himself. It was as if he died for me once again."

Late in this process, his therapist asked him, "How do you

feel with God's just putting up with this?"

"I feel loved," Mike said. "I've said the most unimaginable things to him. And yet it's as if he's saying, 'I'm not going to leave you. I will not give you away.' "

Slowly in this process, Mike lost his old faith, and the despair that went with it.

Confused and at Peace

Despair still attacks Mike, as it does all of us. But the war against debilitating despair has been won, though mop-up operations will continue the rest of his life.

Mike regrets the loss of his marriage. He remains single, with diminishing hopes of remarriage and a family. But he says, "I'd like to get married again. But I'm in my mid-forties now; I realize the odds are against me starting a family at my age. I'm content to remain in this state, if this is what God wants of me."

His ministry continues in San Antonio. The church remains healthy, and Mike's preaching is well received. "I don't have to play games in my preaching anymore. I don't have to pretend that I'm the model Christian, that it's my reputation that's on the line each Sunday. When I preach law, people know that I do so standing under grace. For all of us, that makes obeying Christ much more attractive."

As far as his faith, Mike remains happily confused. When he was cursing God yet not dying, he would ask, *Why isn't God leaving me?* This was not right: be good to God and he'll be good to you; blaspheme God and he'll curse you. But Mike discovered, to his frustration at first, he couldn't make God do anything. As he reflected on it, though, he realized it was the best news yet.

"God was just being God," he says. "That was a breakthrough for me. I didn't have to figure out God anymore. He didn't do anything I could have predicted: no judgment, no quick-fix answers. He was just present. When I had God figured out, I didn't experience him. Now that I don't have him figured out, I experience him."

One more thing: to this day, when Mike finds a spider in his shower, he carefully picks it up, opens his front door, and places it outside.

I am prone to a kind of Captain Ahab syndrome: an obsessive, self-absorbed, grim pursuit to the death of the great white whale of ministry.

— *John Ortberg*

CHAPTER EIGHT

A Cure for Seriousness

When we take our children to the shrine of the Golden Arches, they always lust for the meal that comes with a cheap little prize, a combination christened, in a moment of marketing genius, the Happy Meal. You're not just buying fries, McNuggets, and a dinosaur stamp; you're buying happiness. Their advertisements have convinced my children they have a little McDonald-shaped vacuum in their souls: "Our hearts are restless till they find their rest in a happy meal."

I try to buy off the kids sometimes. I tell them to order only the food and I'll give them a quarter to buy a little toy on their own. But the cry goes up, "I want a Happy Meal." All over the restaurant, people crane their necks to look at the tight-fisted, penny-pinching cheapskate of a parent who would deny a child the meal of great joy.

The problem with the Happy Meal is that the happy wears off, and they need a new fix. No child discovers lasting happiness in just one: "Remember that Happy Meal? What great joy I found there!"

Happy Meals bring happiness only to McDonalds. You ever wonder why Ronald McDonald wears that grin? Twenty billion Happy Meals, that's why.

When you get older, you don't get any smarter; your happy meals just get more expensive.

Not long after we'd had the first public Sunday service at our church, I talked to a friend who pastors a church he helped found thirty years ago. "Savor these days," he advised me. "You'll discover one day that these early days will have been the best years of your life."

I nodded, but inwardly I told myself he must be crazy. The early days are chaos and uncertainty. Someday we will have stability and continuity, we will have security and resources and credibility; we will have arrived. "That's when I'll be happy," I whispered to myself. That's when fulfillment will kick in, when we have arrived.

Saving Face

On the last day I worked with him, the man who mentored me in pastoring said he had two things he wanted me to remember. One of them I've long since forgotten (which means either it was pretty superficial or I'm headed for serious trouble), but the other has stuck with me. "Have fun," he said. "Being in ministry should be fun. If you ever have an extended period in ministry when you're not having fun, it's a warning that something needs to be attended to."

But when I talk to other pastors, fun is usually not high on the list of topics. Anxiety, pressure, anger, and fear get more air time. And when I look at myself, I see stretches of time far too long where joy is not prominent. Are we having fun yet? And if we're not, when will we?

I treasure a classic line I heard in a church I served years ago. One of the staff members didn't smile more than two or three times a year. An old deacon finally asked him, "Pastor X," (not his real name), "are you happy?"

"Yes. Of course."

"Well, tell your face."

Tell your face. I have wondered many times since what my face is trying to tell me about my soul.

There are certain warning lights that indicate when my joy tank is running on fumes. I am prone to a kind of Captain Ahab syndrome: an obsessive, self-absorbed, grim pursuit to the death of the great white whale of ministry.

Some time ago, I was giving our three kids a bath. I'm a busy guy, so I bathe all three at once to save time (I know this will have to change some day, probably when they're in high school). Our oldest child was finished and combing her hair, our youngest was playing with his armada, and our middle child was on drip-dry. I was reviewing my sermon notes (polyphasia, doing multiple things at one time, is a common symptom of joyless ministry).

"Hurry up," I said to our middle child, more out of habit than anything else. She was doing a dance called "Dee Dah Day." This consists of running in a circle, chanting "Dee Dah Day" over and over as in some pagan fertility ritual.

"Hurry up — *Now!*" I said, this time with some anger.

"Why?" she said.

I didn't have an answer. I had nowhere to go, nothing I had to do. I had just become so preoccupied, so addicted to hurry, so grimly task focused, that I was incapable of celebrating a Dee Dah Day moment. I know the day is coming when the Dee Dah Day dance will not be performed again, when I will give a thousand dollars to see it once more, but it will be too late. Impatience, preoccupation, hurry, obsession with church life — these are indications that my joy muscle has seriously atrophied.

The Paradox of Joy

G. K. Chesterton wrote once that it is in paradox that the truth of Christianity emerges most clearly.

For instance, about human nature some say we are essentially eternal spirits; others say we're just highly evolved lumps of clay ("portable plumbing," as one poet says). Christianity holds both extremes simultaneously. The same is true about the Christian view of human nature: it's both pessimistic (human beings are sinful) and optimistic (we can be saved).

Philosophies that try to reduce life or reality to a single theme lose the wild, diverse richness that makes Christianity ring so true. Christianity works at both ends of the canvas and paints a whole picture.

There is a paradox about ministry that, when I hold both ends with passion, helps me to keep a firmer grip on joy. When I let go of one or the other end of this paradox, joy is at risk. The biggest paradox might be this: my work matters immensely, and yet my work doesn't matter at all.

Lightness of Being

Take the second half first. When Theodore Roosevelt went camping with his friend, naturalist William Beebe, they used to sit under the open sky at night and search for a tiny blob of light near the constellation Pegasus and chant together, "That is the Spiral Galaxy in Andromeda. It is as large as our Milky Way. It is one of a hundred million galaxies. It consists of one hundred billion suns, each larger than our sun." Then Roosevelt would say to Beebe, "Now I think we are small enough. Let's go to bed."

For me, this stargazing and perspective-restoration takes place at a retreat center about thirty minutes from my office. I go there once a week and meet with a group in which we reflect on our prayers over the past week. Our lives are connected only through this group. No one in the group is familiar with my church or even my denomination. I have the gift of anonymity, of being with people who will not be impressed by my success or cluck their tongues over my failure. Sometimes just being on the grounds at this center, I am given the gift of solitude — true detachment (at least for a moment or two) from the rewards and punishments of my "world system" that seeks to squeeze me into its mold.

There I get an occasional glimmer of the immensity of God, and I can rejoice in my smallness and enjoy "lightness of being." Then I recognize my most strenuous efforts are the strategical equivalent of a hyperactive three year old helping Julia Child with the cooking. I become a little bit less messianic.

When I let go of this truth, my joy is at risk. Some time ago at a retreat, a group of us who worked on staff together responded to the question "What is the greatest fear in your life?" All of us but one were around age 30, and we all gave roughly the same answer: our biggest fear was "not making a difference."

To a degree, this is probably healthy; impacting people is a good thing. But it became apparent as we talked that much of what fueled this fear was the need for visible, readily apparent success. We were all under the illusion that somewhere out there was a level of success high enough to satisfy this need once and for all.

Anthony Meisel introduces *The Rule of St. Benedict* by noting how one of the goals of Benedictine life was to liberate members of the community from this fear. Since their primary task was union with God, their work was to be evaluated not by "material results" but by "growth in virtue." The Rule intends to free people from the enticements and terrors of the world and its values, from addiction to success and fear of failure, and so learn truly to desire God.

Not that the Rule was always successful, but it made a peace-filled path that tried to evade the danger of obsessing over success. Meisel concludes, "For the man of the twentieth century, such serenity and freedom would be treasure indeed."

In general, I take myself too seriously and God not seriously enough. Joy comes when I get it the other way around.

Manageable, Meaningful Work

The other side of this paradox is that what human beings do is of immense importance.

It's hard for ministers to be convinced of that considering how our culture sometimes perceives us. Garrison Keillor writes about when the mayor of Lake Wobegon, Clint Bunsen, hosted a group of ministers on a tour called, "Meeting the pastoral needs of rural America":

"They got off the bus, and Cliff thought, *Ministers*. Men in their forties mostly, a little thick around the middle, thin on top, puffy hair around the ears, some fish medallions, turtleneck pullovers, earth tones, Hush Puppies; but more than dress, what set them apart was the ministerial eagerness, more eye contact than you were really looking for, a longer handshake, and a little more affirmation than you needed. 'Good to see you, glad you could be here, nice of you to come, we're very honored,' they said to him, although they were guests and he was the host."

The world isn't always impressed with ministers. Yet the doings of the most apparently insignificant person (or store-front pastor) will last when every government and civilization and multinational corporation has been consigned to the ash heap of history. Through people wearing Hush Puppies and fish medallions, through people wearing ephods and robes embroidered with bells and pomegranates, through people as ridiculous as you and me, God has chosen to express himself, to make himself known. That is something I can never take seriously enough.

Joy is not found in ceasing from all effort. We may be prone to base identity overmuch on achievement, but without any achievement there is no identity. There is surely a connection between joy and what we do with our lives.

All human beings seem to have a drive toward growth and mastery. But as Gilbert Brim writes in *Ambition*, "One important source of happiness is working at the right level of challenge, whatever that level might be for each of us. . . . It is the challenge more than the material achievement that brings us happiness. . . . There is the intrinsic satisfaction of achieving a goal itself — having food, health, wealth, love; but, as I will say often, the happiness derived from the achievement itself does not last long. When we win, we rest a moment but then move on; the joy of success is soon gone."

Brim notes that studies indicate major social characteristics like age, gender, education, income, and race combined can account for only about 10 to 15 percent of the variation in happiness among human beings. He writes, "I believe most of the differences between us are caused by our individual actions, by whether we have found a way to live at the level of just manageable difficulty."

This realization has both enlightened me about the futility of thinking any achievement can bring lasting fulfillment, and it also gives me the goal of seeking to live each day at the level of "just manageable difficulty." For me, this varies from day to day; some days just getting out of bed pretty much takes care of it.

At one point, it meant saying no to a terrific educational experience. I didn't want to say no. "But I know you," my wife said. "I see little enough of you as it is already. If you take this on, in addition to everything else, I will get only the leftovers. You won't have enough energy left to give to our relationship, let alone really to enjoy life."

I didn't enjoy that conversation. I like to think that I have unlimited reserves of energy and competence. But I know if I hadn't said no, the only person more miserable than my wife would have been me. (I don't tell her that, because I'm still spending the chips I earned for making the decision "for her.") So I had to cut back to a level of "just manageable difficulty."

Finally then, in my ministry I'm left with the same paradox I see in my daughter's young life. When she marches off to her first day of school, washed and dressed and combed and camcorded with elaborate care, I want to yell at her, "Don't worry about school. Don't worry about A's and B's, about whether or not you get a happy face, about what your class standing is or whether the teacher likes you. Don't carry with you any of those silly anxieties. It doesn't matter! Be free!"

At the same time I want to yell, "You are off now on a great adventure. Now you can ask questions, think great thoughts, discover deep truths that perhaps no mortal creature has ever seen. It is a precious gift, your mind, so don't waste it, don't take it for granted."

Each day as I drive to my office, I expect if I could hear God yelling, he would be yelling something similar to me.

Living the Joy We Preach

Above all, the issue of joy revolves around a question I'm spending more and more time with these days: Is the life I invite people into the life that I'm living?

At a pastor's conference not long ago, I met the main speaker. He talked candidly about his life, and not far beneath the surface he admitted to some burnout and exhaustion, marital strain and personal stress. Nor was this an exceptional time, he said. His view of ministry was that it would take a couple of psychological cornermen to keep repairing him between rounds and sending him back into the ring.

He invited people into a life of peace, joy, and trust, but the reality of life in ministry was hurry, crisis, and fatigue. One got the sense that people were invited to be saved, but if they got deeply enough into ministry, they too would enter into this frenzied lifestyle, all for the purpose of producing more of the "saved" who would ultimately look like them.

This stood in vivid contrast to a man who has written extensively on spiritual life and is also in high demand as a speaker. During an evening I spent with him in his home, he never hurried. The phone rang, and he just let it ring because he was with another person; he was not its slave. He never looked at his watch; he never dropped a name. He appeared to have no place else to go and nothing else to do even though he was a busy man and this night was of no "strategic value" to his career.

He gave the impression that he had gained the power to simply live in each moment with God as it unfolded. The life he writes about, the life he invites people to lead, is the life he himself lives.

Ultimately, then, joy in ministry is a product of a joyous relationship with Christ, nurtured in prayer and worship. It is there that Jesus says to us, "Take my flesh for your bread, and my blood for your wine, and you will finally find food that can nourish your soul. Take my words, and you will find life. For the meal of sacrifice and death — of ministry — is in fact the meal of great joy. It is not just a happy meal; it is the meal of hope, the last supper before the entrance into the kingdom. And the little prize inside, the gift that costs everything and costs nothing, that is worth so little and yet valued beyond price — the little prize is your soul."

And to some of us, as a gift beyond comprehension, he entrusts the task of delivering this meal to his children, to our brothers and sisters. "And remember," he says, "it is a happy meal. So be happy."

And tell your face.

Part 2
Sexual Snares

Given the right circumstances, the best among us is capable of the most unimaginable sins.

— *Richard Exley*

CHAPTER NINE

Handling Sexual Temptation

Few things in life are more painful than a moral failure. This truth was driven home to me afresh when a fellow pastor sought my counsel. Hardly had I closed the office door before he fell to his knees sobbing. When he was able to compose himself, he spilled his dark secret.

He was not an evil man; he never intended to become involved in sexual sin. It started innocently with morning coffee at a nearby convenience store. One morning while sipping his coffee, he found himself browsing through the pornographic magazines.

A few mornings later he purchased one, and days later, another.

His story shows an all too familiar progression: from maga-zines to X-rated videos to porno theaters to securing the services of a prostitute. This degenerating progression didn't happen overnight; it took months. After each step he told himself he would go no farther.

As you might imagine, he lived in a self-made hell: moments of lustful pleasure followed by hours of shame, days and weeks of regret. Yet even in his shame, he was drawn irresistibly toward the very thing he hated. His desperate prayers seemed powerless against the demons within. He lived in secrecy and fear: *What if someone sees me? What if my wife or someone from the church finds out?*

Then his worst fears were realized: he contracted a sexually transmitted disease and infected his wife with it. At least it wasn't AIDS, but now he was forced to burden her with his seedy secret so she could receive treatment.

His story is not unique. With increasing frequency, ministers are falling prey to sexual temptation. Of the 300 pastors who re-sponded to a recent LEADERSHIP survey, 19 percent admitted to having either an affair or inappropriate sexual contact with people other than their spouses. Nine percent confessed to having sexual intercourse with people other than their spouses.

As disconcerting as the statistics may be, we shouldn't be surprised ministers are prone to sexual temptation. For some, like my friend, it comes in the form of lust. For others, it is more subtle: sexual temptation is rooted in virtue not vice. What begins as legiti-mate ministry — a shared project, compassionate listening, the giving of comfort — becomes an emotional bonding, which ulti-mately leads to an illicit affair.

While sexual temptation can strike randomly, many ministers seem to be most vulnerable during mid-life. (Since my experience and most of my research in this area has been with males, I'm assuming a male pastor for this chapter.) He reaches mid-life only to discover that, for all his achievements, he still feels unfulfilled. He is especially susceptible to affirmation from the opposite sex. Being appreciated as a man, and not just a minister, feels good. He doesn't intend to commit adultery, but affirmation can, and often does, lead to affection, which in turn leads to inappropriate intimacy.

Others fall prey to their own success. Subconsciously they've come to believe the laws of God, which apply to ordinary people, can be amended to suit their lifestyles. This self-deception doesn't happen instantaneously; it's the product of a series of small compromises, which are often revealed by the way the minister treats the perks afforded by his ministry. First he *accepts* them, then he *expects* them, then he *demands* them, and finally he *abuses* them. Once integrity is compromised in any area, it is only a matter of time until the whole is affected.

Yet ministerial infidelity is not inevitable — 91 percent of those responding to LEADERSHIP's survey indicated they had not committed adultery! We should not, however, assume they aren't tempted. Every pastor will be subject from time to time to some degree of sexual temptation. Yet there are some effective strategies to combat it.

Assuming the Worst

Given the right circumstances, the best among us is capable of the most unimaginable sins. The sooner we come to grips with this painful truth, the sooner we can be about the business of overcoming temptation.

Recognizing our propensity for sin is the first step. The apostle Paul warns us of the danger of overconfidence, "If you think you are standing firm, be careful that you don't fall" (1 Cor. 10:12).

Overconfidence can set us up for a moral failure. The two most common ways are spiritual naiveté and risktaking.

The spiritually naive pastor is simply out of touch with his own humanity. Succumbing to a sexual sin is to him inconceivable. Spending extended hours in personal ministry with a member of the opposite sex, even in unsupervised settings, is nothing to him. When the inevitable temptation comes, it blind-sides him. The aftermath devastates him, and he finds living with himself impossible. Usually he takes the initiative in confessing his sin to his wife and church officials.

The risktaker, on the other hand, is an adventurer. He is addicted to danger and excitement, and like a moth drawn to a flame, he is drawn to the heat of temptation. He recognizes the possibility of a moral failure — in fact, it is that very possibility that excites him. But he believes he can handle it. The risktaker overestimates his moral resolve and usually succumbs to temptation in short order.

The spiritually naive pastor and the risk-taking pastor, who have almost nothing in common, share a fatal flaw — overconfidence. And like Peter, who boasted he would never deny Jesus but later found himself weeping bitterly after doing just that, they too have become victims of their own presumption.

Offensive Maneuvers

As a young pastor, I soon discovered my own feet of clay. Although my motives were pure, at least as far as I knew, I repeatedly found myself confronted with inappropriate thoughts and desires. Sometimes the temptations came upon me because of my own wandering mind. Other times, the source was troubled counselees or distraught parishioners who became emotionally attached to me. Keeping my feelings, and theirs, in check required enormous amounts of spiritual and emotional energy, energy better spent cultivating my marriage or practicing spiritual disciplines.

For several years, I simply accepted these disconcerting and distracting emotions as inevitable — the price of being an effective pastor and counselor. I prayed and hoped these temptations would in time fade. But as the years passed, they grew in intensity. I finally concluded that if I didn't do something quickly, I too might become a casualty of immorality.

With renewed determination, I turned my attention to my methods of ministry. Much to my chagrin, I discovered I was creating many of my problems, not deliberately but out of ignorance. Once I understood what was happening, I implemented a number of guidelines to protect both the counselee and myself.

For instance, I determined I would not counsel with anyone more than six times. If the situation required more sessions, I referred the person to a Christian counselor, someone who specialized in the field. Not only did this protect me from an unhealthy emotional attachment, it also assured the counselee of gaining the best available help.

When I do counsel, the sessions are always pastoral and professional, never chummy. I see counselees only in my office and only when my secretary or other staff members are at the church office. I refuse to counsel a woman regarding sexual matters unless her spouse is present. Nor do I telephone a counselee between sessions "to see how she is doing."

And I pray for counselees only on the day I am going to see them. This serves two purposes.

First, it protects me from burnout; it helps me compartmentalize their needs, freeing me from the combined weight of concern for several clients.

Second, it protects me from an unhealthy emotional bonding. Being compassionate by nature, pastors genuinely feel responsible for the spiritual and emotional well-being of those to whom they minister. There is always a temptation to overinvest in their lives, creating an unhealthy dependency. When we pray for our counselees daily, we only reinforce our overdeveloped sense of responsibility. As incongruent as it seems, prayer itself can become an incubator in which sexual temptation is hatched. Praying for someone whom you're attracted to only fills your heart and mind with fodder for the enemy.

Scanning Your Radar

Succumbing to sexual sin is seldom sudden. Rather it is the culmination of a series of small temptations. Recognizing it when it first whispers its beguiling suggestions is imperative. In his book, *As For Me and My House,* Walter Wangerin, Jr., calls this first subtle temptation a moment of "maybe":

"Early on in an extramarital friendship there often comes a moment of 'maybe.' Even when that friendship is altogether innocent, your friend may send the signal, or you may sense the feeling, of further possibility. It occurs in a glance more meaningful than mere friends exchange. It arises from a touch, a hug, a brushing of flesh that tingled rather more than you expected — and you remembered the sensation. . . . In that moment nothing more is communicated than this: our friendship could turn into something else. Neither of you need say, or even think, what that 'something else' might be . . . it is precisely here that the drama toward adultery begins. Whether it also ends here, or whether it continues hereafter, is a terribly critical question. For a door has opened up.

"If, in this moment, you do nothing at all, then you enter the door. If you make no decision (privately but consciously) to close the door and carefully to restrict this relationship, the drama continues. For though a promise has not been made in the moment of 'maybe,' it hasn't been denied either. And though you may not yet love each other, neither have you said no to love. You permit, by making no decision at all, the 'maybe.' And 'maybe' takes on a life of its own."

Wangerin concludes, "When a desire is born in us, we have a choice. When it exists still in its infancy, we have a choice. We can carefully refuse its existence altogether, since it needs our complicity to exist. . . . Or else we can attend to it, think about it, fantasize it into greater existence — feed it! . . . But if we do the latter, if we give it attention in our souls, soon we will be giving it our souls. We've lost free will and the opportunity to choose. The desire itself overpowers us, commanding action, demanding satisfaction."

Temptation is so subtle that recognizing a moment of "maybe" isn't always easy, especially if we're inclined to rationalize. We reason that ministry requires sensitivity, support, and care. And it does. But there is a point where concern becomes more than pastoral, where you find yourself meeting her emotional needs — and she, yours — needs that should be met only by one's spouse. Although nothing sexually inappropriate has been done, we are nonetheless guilty of emotional adultery at that point. And if immediate steps are not taken, a full-blown affair is only a matter of time.

The earliest warning signals of emotional entanglement include but are not limited to

1. *A growing fascination with this person*, when she regularly intrudes upon your thoughts, even when you are with your wife

and family.

2. A heightened sense of anticipation as her appointment draws near, when you find yourself looking forward to "ministry" opportunities when you can legitimately be alone with her, or when you create church projects so the two of you can be together.

3. A growing desire to confide in her, when you are tempted to share with her the frustrations and disappointments in your marriage.

4. An increased sense of responsibility for her happiness and well-being, when you think more about her needs than the needs of your wife and family.

5. Emotional distancing from your spouse, when you keep from your wife your secret thoughts and feelings for her.

The moment an early warning signal is tripped, we must act with ruthless urgency. As Thomas à Kempis pointed out in the *Imitation of Christ*, "The only time to stop temptation is at the first point of recognition. If one begins to argue and engage in a hand-to-hand combat, temptation almost always wins the day."

Strong Words

In the midst of temptation, especially sexual temptation, our emotions are not reliable moral compasses. The heart is too easily deceived and too deceiving. Only the infallible Word of God can be trusted. It should always be our first and last defense against the deceiver, who seeks to destroy both our souls and ministries.

The Word of God exposes the lies of the enemy for what they are. When we're tempted to believe our situations are unique, and therefore exempt from the laws of God that govern others, the Scriptures remind us, "For of this you can be sure: No immoral, impure or greedy person — such a man is an idolater — has any inheritance in the kingdom of Christ and of God. . . . Because of such things God's wrath comes on those who are disobedient" (Eph. 5:5–6).

When we feel powerless to resist temptation, the Bible says, "God is faithful; he will not let you be tempted beyond what you can bear. But when you are tempted, he will also provide a way out so that you can stand up under it" (1 Cor. 10:13).

When the enemy tries to isolate us, to make us believe no one, least of all God, understands the pull of lust, the Scriptures declare, "For we do not have a high priest who is unable to sympathize with our weaknesses, but we have one who has been tempted in every way, just as we are — yet without sin" (Heb. 4:15).

And when tempted to rationalize, to say to ourselves, "No one will ever know," the Scriptures scream out a warning: "Do not be deceived: God cannot be mocked. A man reaps what he sows. The one who sows to please his sinful nature, from that nature will reap destruction" (Gal. 6:7–8).

As Proverbs wisely says, "Can a man scoop fire into his lap without his clothes being burned? Can a man walk on hot coals without his feet being scorched? So is he who sleeps with another man's wife; no one who touches her will go unpunished. . . . A man who commits adultery lacks judgment; whoever does so destroys himself. Blows and disgrace are his lot, and his shame will never be wiped away" (Prov. 6:27–29, 32–33).

The minister who is serious about overcoming sexual temptation will find great help by living in the Word of God, meditating on it day and night, memorizing it. His prayer will then be that of the Psalmist: "I have hidden your word in my heart that I might not sin against you" (Ps. 119:11).

The Light of Friendship

Temptation, which flourishes in secret, somehow loses much of its mesmerizing power when confessed and exposed to Christian love. That which seems so alluring in the privacy of the imagination is revealed for what it is in the transparency of confession. So, we should expose temptation immediately. Tell your wife, a Christian brother, a fellow minister, whomever — but get it out into the light.

Gordon MacDonald, pastor of Grace Chapel in Lexington, Massachusetts, and author of *Ordering Your Private World* and *Rebuilding Your Broken World*, speaks as a pastor who has experienced the tragic consequences of a moral failure. In an interview with

Christianity Today following his public confession of adultery, he explained, but did not excuse, his behavior. One of the contributing factors, he said, was a lack of accountability — friendships in which one man regularly looks another man in the eyes and asks hard questions about his moral life: his lust, his ambitions, his ego.

I can testify to the redemptive power of accountability. Some years ago, I began to sense in a counseling session a strong attraction to the woman I was counseling. When the session was over, I immediately went to my associate pastor and confessed my feelings. When I did, I was liberated from their seductive power. While secret they were strangely seductive, but in the light of open confession, they became evil and repugnant. I also asked him to check up on me, to ensure I did not allow myself to become emotionally involved with this woman.

Limiting the Risks

Not a few ministers have fallen prey to sexual temptation because of poor judgment. In ministry, a certain amount of risk is unavoidable, but the minister who repeatedly exposes himself to tempting situations is tempting fate.

For instance, one minister friend will not accept outside speaking engagements unless his wife, or a Christian brother, travels with him. Why? Because the few times he has traveled alone, he struggled with sexual temptation. He now refuses to travel alone.

Another pastor was tempted repeatedly as he counseled women. He prayed about it and sought the counsel of a trusted colleague, but nothing seemed to help. Finally he made the difficult decision to limit his counseling to men only. His decision raised some eyebrows — some thought he was shirking his duties. But he has stood by it. As a result, his spiritual life blossomed. An added benefit was that the lay counseling program at the church began training mature Christian women to counsel with younger women.

A Time to Run Away

Rare though they are, all of us have heard of ministers who, through no fault of their own, were confronted with compromising situations. One pastor responded to an emergency phone call only to be greeted, just inside the door, by a nearly nude woman with something other than pastoral care on her mind. Another pastor, while his wife and children were away, was visited unexpectedly by a seductive young woman.

In such instances, we have only one option — run for our life!

Joseph is our example: "Now Joseph was well-built and handsome, and after a while his master's wife took notice of Joseph and said, 'Come to bed with me!' But he refused. 'My master has withheld nothing from me except you, because you are his wife. How then could I do such a wicked thing and sin against God?' And though she spoke to Joseph day after day, he refused to go to bed with her or even be with her. One day he went into the house to attend to his duties, and none of the household servants was inside. She caught him by his cloak and said, 'Come to bed with me!' *But he left his cloak in her hand and ran out of the house*" (emphasis mine), (Gen. 39:6–12).

The power of temptation is such that unless a stake is driven into its heart immediately, it may well overwhelm us. Kings have renounced their thrones, saints their God, and spouses their lifetime partners. People have been known to sell their souls, jobs, reputations, children, marriage — they have literally chucked everything for a brief moment of sexual pleasure.

But with Christ, everything is possible, including the resisting of this temptation: "But you, man of God, flee from all this, and pursue righteousness, godliness, faith, love, endurance and gentleness. Fight the good fight of faith. Take hold of the eternal life to which you were called when you made your good confession in the presence of many witnesses" (1 Tim. 6:11–12).

*Susan felt as if God were telling her, "Don't stop. Your
life and marriage depend on your keeping on, one step at
a time, no matter the pain."*

— Mark Galli

CHAPTER TEN

An Overlooked Casualty of a "Victimless" Sin

As they drove home, light from street lamps and store signs
flickered across the dashboard and over their faces. Susan Hyde,
slight with pale red hair, sat across from her husband, Brad, an
associate pastor of Calvary Assembly of God in Regina, Saskatche-
wan. They were returning from a birthday party for one of the
women of the church, another activity in another hurried week.

"We should go to the new Pizza Hut," Brad said.

Now? thought Susan. Brad had mentioned he wanted to try it
out, but she was stuffed from the party, and she didn't think Brad

needed more to eat. "We can't. We're paying a babysitter. We need to get home."

"No, let's go to Pizza Hut."

Susan didn't get it. It was already past ten. But she was in no mood for one of their fights. Maybe he just wanted to be alone together. *That would be nice*, she thought.

Inside the restaurant, the smell of fresh upholstery and newly-laid carpet hit Susan before her eyes adjusted to the dim lighting. Brad pushed himself into one side of a booth, and Susan slipped into the other. Except for a couple across the room, the place was empty.

They ordered a pizza, something with "little sausage things that Brad likes," Susan later recalled. When the waiter left, Brad put his hands on the table and leaned forward. Susan realized there was an agenda.

"Susan, do you remember what you were telling me earlier, about what you talked to David about today?"

She felt a fight coming on. David was her counselor. She had convinced Brad to go with her for a while, but he had laid down a condition: "We're not going to talk about anything sexual. Nothing." And when he first talked to David, he had said, "We're not going to talk about sex. We don't need to. Everything's great. There are no problems there." Still, Brad had stopped going after a couple of months. That morning, Susan had talked to David about her unhappiness with their sex life. Before the party, she had mentioned it to Brad.

"There's something I've been wanting to tell you for a long time," Brad continued.

Susan raced to figure out what he was going to say. His round face and dark eyes were nearly lost in the dimness. He didn't seem angry. *Maybe this is it*, she thought.

For months, she had been expecting to hear about an affair, especially after one winter day when Brad brought home a copy of *The Myth of the Greener Grass* by J. Allan Petersen, a book about marital infidelity. The long hours, the lack of sexual interest — it only made sense. She narrowed down the possible candidates to one or two church women with whom Brad had been especially demonstrative. After Brad admitted his affair, she had decided, she would still love him. It would be hard, but it would be okay. She would find out what he had done, with whom, why. They would change churches, of course, and start all over again. But it would be okay; at least it would be out in the open.

"All these years," Brad continued, "I've been struggling with something." Susan's hands felt moist. She braced to hear a woman's name. *Lord, I need grace. Whatever he says, I just have to think about grace, and that it will be okay.*

"All these years, it's been pornography."

Susan couldn't breathe. Brad stared at the Formica table and rubbed his hands back and forth. Susan twisted her napkin and fought with herself: *I can't cry in a restaurant.*

Not-So-Perfect Marriage

By that night, Brad and Susan had been married for just over eleven years. The first year of marriage was a long honeymoon, and the next three a blur: Susan bore three children in three years (and two months, and six days, she says).

By the time they moved to Regina five years into marriage, something was missing. They rarely did things together — Brad had his church activities, and Susan, hers. Brad read his books, Susan, hers.

They rarely talked about their relationship. When they did, they fought, not for an hour but for two days.

"I find our relationship empty," Susan would begin. "Don't you?"

"What do you want from me?" he would reply.

"Well, the same thing you give to people at church. I want that for me."

Brad gave the best part of himself at church, often for eighty hours a week. He looked parishioners in the eyes and displayed obvious pastoral concern. When they came to the front of the church at the end of worship, he gently encouraged them and prayed for them. But he would come home drained; he had nothing left for her and the children.

"You've got to understand," Brad would argue, "this is for the kingdom of God. When we were called into the ministry, we knew it would mean sacrifices."

"But who's doing most of the sacrificing? I don't mind not having lots of money and having to work part time, but it seems ministry gets the best of everything!"

Then they would fight about whether it was godly to be driven, if that was really furthering the kingdom.

Susan worried about what Brad's schedule was doing to their three children. During one feverish period, Brad had missed a string of family dinners. When he finally broke free one evening — with the understanding he would have to return to the church later — 6-year-old Katy, with childlike sincerity, greeted him, "Dad, this is such a surprise. This is just great! I'm so glad that you took time to visit us!"

Susan and Brad also fought about sex. Brad just didn't seem interested.

"Brad, why don't we ever make love? What's the problem?"

"Nothing. I'm happy the way things are. You're just imagining a problem."

"I don't think so. I think we have to deal with it."

"Then, deal with it!"

"Brad, is there a problem with me, something that stops you from wanting to make love to me?"

"No."

"How come you can go for days and days and not feel any stress or lack of fulfillment?"

"What do you want from me?"

"Isn't it obvious?"

"Listen: stop looking to me to meet all your needs!"

Susan was dumbfounded — where else was she supposed to

go to satisfy her sexual desires?

They battled over these issues so much that Susan felt they had memorized each other's lines; they didn't even need each other to fight.

Not all was misery. When they avoided talking about their relationship, which was most of the time, life could be good: slow walks together through the nearby ravine, rounds of family wrestling on their queen-size bed, family trips to Blue Lake for hotdog roasts. They probably seemed a model pastor's family to the congregation.

And it wasn't as if they never made love. It just wasn't as much as Susan wished, and sometimes not as Susan liked. Some nights she wondered if it was to her that Brad was making love.

Many nights, after he rolled over and went to sleep, she sat up in bed and thought, *What is wrong? Our marriage is so empty.* She would rehearse a litany: *His shirts are always ironed. His meals are on time. I support him in church work even though I don't like him being there all the time.* She often silently wept, *Why this emptiness?*

Still, she admired Brad: his passion to do something significant for God, his bottomless reservoirs of energy, his ability to put on a happy face no matter what they were going through. She often wondered if Brad was right. Maybe she was the weak one. Maybe she needed to stop whining. On their tenth anniversary, in fact, it looked as if things were getting better after all.

Brad went all out. He found a sitter for the kids and rented a plush room at a freshly remodeled hotel in downtown Regina; millions had been spent to capture the golden aura of the 1890s. *Gorgeous* was the common description of it. The evening was a complete surprise for Susan.

As they made their way through the lobby, Susan craned her head at yards of lace and rich, dark green fabric covering everything in the Victorian aura. When Brad opened their room, on the bed were a dozen red roses. *This is perfect*, she thought.

They went downstairs and had a leisurely supper. Susan was feeling like a woman, a woman someone wanted. As they lingered over tea, she thought, *Maybe there's hope here.*

When they returned to their room, Susan took off her shoes,

loosened her belt, and sat on the bed. Brad walked past her and picked up the remote control to the TV. He started flipping channels; he hit on an adult channel and started watching a graphic sex scene.

Susan blinked and then turned away. *Surely he'll flip it off.* Brad kept watching. She walked over and turned it off. His eyes on the blank screen, Brad punched the remote control, and the TV popped back on.

Susan felt sick. She wanted desperately to avoid a fight, but she couldn't just stand there. "Brad, I don't feel comfortable with that on," she said calmly. Then she shut it off again. Brad turned it back on.

Sadness enveloped Susan; she walked into the bathroom, put on her nightgown, and crawled into bed. Brad watched awhile and then joined her, the TV still flickering the obscene images. He stroked and kissed her; soon he was making love to her. For Susan it wasn't the perfect evening anymore.

Brad's Story

The waiter set down the pizza and the dinner plates; they clanked on the table. Susan looked across the room; Brad gazed at the steaming cheese.

"Is everything okay?" the waiter asked.

"Yeah, everything's fine," Brad said.

The waiter walked away, and Brad started talking: he'd been clean about six months, but he'd had a problem since childhood when his brother brought some porn magazines into the house; after they married, he thought he was through with a phase, but since they moved to Regina, it had become a problem again.

Susan counted the eight wedges of pizza. *He wasn't eating any pizza! What would the waiter think?* She took a bite, but the warm cheese just lay lumped in her mouth.

Brad said he used pornography mostly when she would go away for a weekend, and then he would binge. Sometimes when he was angry with her, he would go to a local store, buy a *Penthouse* or whatever, and take it somewhere and masturbate.

Susan stared at a button on Brad's shirt. *If I look at his face, I'm going to cry.*

"I've been wanting to tell you this for a long time," he said, "but I didn't know when the time would be right. I'm telling you now."

Susan swallowed hard and started crying.

The waiter returned. "Is everything all right?" Only two bites were missing from the pizza; their glasses were still full.

"Yes, everything's all right," Brad said. The waiter left.

Susan dried her eyes with a napkin. "We've got to go home. We can't stay here."

Brad motioned the waiter back and asked him to box up the pizza. The waiter leaned over. "Is there a problem?"

What do you think? Susan thought. *I'm crying. We've not eaten a thing!*

"No," Brad said. "Nothing's wrong with the food."

On the drive home, Susan kept dabbing her eyes and cheeks. After paying the sitter, who walked herself home next door, Susan went to their bedroom and fell on their bed. She started sobbing. Brad sat beside her.

"It's all right," Susan said. "I'm glad you told me. I just wasn't expecting to hear 'pornography.' "

That started a long conversation, mostly Brad talking; he told her about what he'd discovered about himself over the last few months.

He had discovered his anger, for one. That April, as part of a masters degree class, he participated in a small group. The group of pastors and seminary students were asked what made them angry. When it was Brad's turn, he blurted out, "There's a lot of stuff! Church people make me angry. There's one deacon — I'd like to walk up to him and tell him to go straight to hell!" Brad was as startled as the rest of the group, but in the following weeks, he realized that though outwardly he played the gracious and patient pastor, inside he was a "seething cesspool of foul language and anger."

He had recognized his drivenness — how the memory of his dad's lectures ("Consider the ant, O sluggard") and his religious culture (which applauded eighty-hour work weeks as sacrifice for the kingdom) had wedded his yearning for approval. He had desperately hoped, by heroic labors for the church, to become acceptable to others, to God, to himself. The pressure had been enormous and had partly led to his fascination with the smiling, willing, accepting women of *Penthouse* and *Oui*.

As far as pornography, he admitted that his rationalizations ("It's harmless; I'm not hurting anyone") were self-deceptions. He had taken the intimacy and passion to be reserved for Susan and had squandered it on pictures of naked women and on masturbation. Worse, he was being racked with guilt and self-recrimination. Whenever he got close to God, he thought, *Brad, just who do you think you are? Don't kid yourself. You're vile. You don't deserve God.*

The last domino fell when one afternoon in his office he watched a video, an interview between Christian psychologist James Dobson and Ted Bundy, the mass murderer. Bundy said that his killing spree had been nurtured by years of using pornography. Brad suddenly saw that the same evil lay in him, and he was overcome with remorse.

A colleague tapped on the door, stuck his head in, and glibly asked what Brad was doing. "Why don't you shut the door and sit down," Brad said. And he confessed to him his addiction to pornography, how it had been at the core of his life, how it had blocked him from getting close to God and his wife.

That was just a few days before this night, which was already into the early hours of the next day. A pile of tissues lay next to Susan. There seemed to be nothing more for each to say. Susan's head ached, and her eyes and cheeks burned.

Brad said, "I'll go brush my teeth, and you can get ready for bed."

Susan suddenly felt awkward. It didn't seem right to sleep together, but they had no spare rooms. Her mind raced as to what to do.

In a few minutes, Brad returned and sat on the edge of the

bed. "Honey, this may seem strange, but I really need to make love to you tonight."

Susan took a deep breath. *Yes, it is strange. If I ever needed grace, it's right now.*

Somewhere between brushing her teeth, washing her face, and putting on her nightgown, she found the grace she needed.

Rapid Improvements

The next morning, Brad made another odd request. For some weeks, Susan had planned to take the kids and spend the weekend with her parents. It was Friday, and she was going to leave that afternoon.

"When you come back on Sunday night," Brad said, "you've got to ask me if I've used pornography. I don't want to put you in the place of having to do this all the time. But this time, you must ask." When she returned, she asked, and he told her.

After his family left, Brad had said to himself, "I know exactly where I am right now." Before he returned to work, he went to a park to read his Bible, but after a few minutes put it down. He just didn't feel like reading it. "But what do I feel?" he asked himself.

"I feel lonely. I miss my family," he muttered. He saw again how much he had used pornography to cover his pain.

He knew now that it was a question of appetite: *I know I'm lonely and have a hunger for diversion,* he thought. So after work, he decided to rent a decent video, one that would allow him some healthy diversion.

He walked to a local store, which happened to be the store where he had rented X-rated movies. *Brad, you're a fool to go into this store,* he thought. *Go to a different one.*

"Don't be silly," he said to himself. "I'm through with that. I'm going to rent a decent video."

He started looking through the videos, but his eyes kept moving right. A large movie poster cordoned off the adult-movie section, but through a two-inch gap between the poster and wall he could see some of the video boxes with their flesh-filled covers. A battle ensued:

"Brad, have one for the road. You're going to move on now; you're going to be free from it. You already told your wife."

"No."

"Go ahead. Just get one. It won't hurt anyone."

"No!"

"Then get an R-rated comedy. How can you be responsible for a few errant breasts?"

"Maybe. . . . No, I won't."

"What's the harm?"

He stood there for nearly fifteen minutes as this inner war raged. He wondered what the proprietor was thinking. Then he thought to pray silently, *Lord, what am I going to do?*

Brad said it was as if the Lord said, "Whatever you rent, Brad, I will watch it with you tonight."

That startled him. He couldn't very well watch something X-rated with the Lord next to him on the couch, he reasoned. With that, he turned and walked out of the store. He arrived home pretty beat up. But he told Susan he felt as if angels came and ministered to him.

Susan felt she was going to like the new Brad.

Alone Again

The week following, the dam burst. Brad shared his addiction with another staff member, who in turn confessed to Brad the same struggles. Over the next few days, four different people came to Brad for counseling, each confessing a battle with pornography. Some days Brad spent his whole day talking about pornography.

Susan spent her days trying to figure out the emotions rushing through her. There were flashes of anger — about what, she couldn't exactly figure out — yet mostly a desire to forgive. God was obviously working in Brad's life; she needn't spoil his recovery by dumping her anger on him. She wanted Brad to know that she had forgiven him.

Suddenly, fourteen days after his confession, Brad came home and announced, "I'm done dealing with it. I feel peace about it. It's all dealt with. I'm done with it."

Susan was incredulous. "How can you say that? We've struggled with this issue for six years. We can't be over with it in two weeks."

"What do you want from me?"

"I want you to be there, to help work this out."

"I've done everything I can. I've confessed it to God. I've confessed it to you. I've told the senior pastor and our counselor. What else do you want from me?"

"I can forgive six years of fighting and feeling like an idiot and thinking it was all me. But we need to pick up the pieces. We need to rebuild."

"I don't want to talk about it anymore. There's nothing more to say."

Susan felt checkmated. *I haven't even begun to say all the things I need to say to you.* But she didn't argue. Brad had made such progress. She didn't want to make him angry. She didn't want him to think she hadn't forgiven him.

What scared Susan more was Brad's reluctance to become accountable. Brad had never promised he wouldn't look at pornography again; Susan was enough of a realist not to expect that. But he had promised he would find someone to hold him accountable, so that if he did fall, he could recover immediately. For the next three months, as gently as she could, she kept reminding him of his promise.

"Brad, have you found somebody to talk to?"

"No, I don't need to."

"Brad, you need to. What are you telling the people who come in for counseling about pornography? Don't you tell them you'll hold them accountable? Who's holding you accountable?"

"I don't need anybody. I'm clean. You need to know that."

"Yes, I need to know that, Brad. But if they need to be held accountable, why the different set of rules for you?"

"I don't want to talk about it."

And the conversation would cease. It took three months before Brad relented.

Long before that, however, Susan had begun to feel isolated.

After Brad confessed, she had mentioned she needed to talk to another pastor or another woman about her feelings. At first, Brad refused: "Don't, please! You can't trust anybody, and if this gets out, my job could be in jeopardy."

Soon he relented and said she could talk with the senior pastor. But when Brad made the initial contact, he refused: "I don't counsel spouses of colleagues. It just gets too complicated."

David, their counselor, thought Susan might find help in the *Leadership* article, "The War Within," about a pastor's struggle with pornography. She searched the article for his wife's feelings, seeking just one word of how she felt — her anger at her husband, her hatred of the women who bared themselves. Nothing.

Brad arranged for her to talk with a woman elder in the church. But after the woman and Susan got together, the woman said, "I don't get it. What's the big attraction about pornography? And why is it so available?" She turned it into a moral issue.

All the while, Brad was receiving encouragement. Staff members reminded him that his sins were covered, that he was in their prayers, that he would make it. No one said a thing to Susan. She had no one to talk with — now not even her husband.

So, she grieved alone with her journal: Why had Brad taken all those years to "discover" his anger and his drivenness? Why hadn't he listened to her? All those years — wasted.

And when he did reveal his turmoil, it had been to relative strangers, not to her.

She recalled the afternoon Brad talked to his colleague in his office. Brad was supposed to take off work early and do something with her and the kids. She kept having the secretary buzz him while she tried to keep the kids entertained. "Just a few things to wrap up." "Be right there." "Just a couple more minutes." Put on hold while he shared his deepest secret with someone else.

It wasn't as if she had been insensitive. Susan remembered the weeks after Brad's pastor had put him in charge of a city-wide anti-pornography campaign, a few months before he confessed to her. Brad made speeches in Sunday school and church. He organized petitions and planned boycotts. And he seemed even more distant and cool and agitated than ever.

One night as they lay in bed, Brad said, "Are you ever scared that you'll be found out?"

"Found out about what, Brad?" He stared at the ceiling. "That you're not a good minister?" Brad shut his eyes. "You're a good minister, Brad. You love the people. If anything, you give them too much. But you err on the side of being good, not on the side of being bad."

"But would you be scared if they found out?"

"Brad, what are you scared of?"

But no matter how gently or carefully she probed, he never revealed himself to her.

Now, as the weeks turned into months, she wondered how the marriage was going to make it. She wondered how she was going to make it.

As she journaled, she kept groping for words, for images that expressed her feelings. One day, she remembered a bitter winter night years earlier.

In Bible college, she and Brad had helped lead a children's ministry. The ministry team of six drove three hours to a church where the children gathered. To get there, they crossed a bridgeless river. Most of the year, they took the ferry; in winter, after the river froze, cars simply drove across.

One winter night, halfway home, they hit a fierce storm. The temperature dropped to 40 degrees below zero; the wind chill took it to 60 below. No tail lights led them, and no headlights came at them — they seemed to be the last car on the road. Their own headlights illumined only the driving snow ahead.

As they crossed the frozen river, the car hung up in a depression. Brad got out to examine the situation. They would need a tow;

someone would need to walk to get help.

About a quarter mile ahead, they saw a house. Brad and Susan volunteered to go. They walked gingerly over the ice; the cold bit through their jackets. Finally, they stepped onto the porch and pounded on the door. No answer. They called out, "Is anyone home?" No answer. They turned and trudged back to the car and warmed themselves.

On a hill about a half-mile behind, they spotted another house, this one with lights shining through the windows. They were sure someone was home. But half a mile, through that cold wind.

Brad and Susan warmed themselves a little longer then stepped out of the car and faced another icy gust. They plodded over the river; they trudged up the hill, holding on to one another. They didn't dare stop to rest; slowly they made their way to the lighted home.

That was how Susan now felt. August to December was a wintry time. But she also sensed God telling her, "Susan, don't stop. Your life and marriage depend on your keeping on, step by step, no matter the pain."

Angry Love

Loneliness wasn't the only bitterness she tasted. She was also beginning to see the depth of her anger.

In a rare moment in early August, Brad had revealed some disturbing things. Once, he said, he had gone to a store near the church and had looked through the adult magazines. When he walked out, he looked to his left: there stood a member of the church. She had walked by the store but hadn't turned in.

Brad thought, *She could have easily turned left, walked into the store to buy some gum or something, and you'd have been standing there.*

"That's right!" Susan now muttered to herself. If he had been caught, the whole family would have been humiliated. He could have lost his job. Then what would they have done? He risked all that to glance at trash!

She recalled all the years Brad had made her feel so stupid, as if everything were her fault. She remembered Brad saying, "Your clothes are too dark; I want you to wear brighter clothes." And "Why don't you wear bigger earrings?" And "Why don't you use more makeup?"

At the time, she couldn't understand why he wasn't satisfied with her. Still, she wore bigger earrings and shorter dresses and tighter blouses. *Maybe he will spend more time at home. Maybe he'll want to make love.* Now she boiled at Brad's demands and her naiveté.

More than anger, though, Susan was plagued with self-doubt. For years she had fretted about what was wrong with her — what about her turned Brad off? Now she discovered that when it came to a choice between her flesh-and-blood and a glossy photo, she lost.

Sometimes she wished he'd had an affair. Instead of one woman, there had been hundreds who had passed through their bedroom. At least with another woman, Susan could compete. Brad would have eventually discovered another woman's flaws. But how was she supposed to compete with picture-perfect fantasies? She wasn't built like them; she didn't smile like them.

Her confidence was shaken. She and Brad went to the mall one evening, and as they entered the main door, they were confronted by a six-foot-high billboard: on it was pictured a woman selling underwear, wearing only a low-cut bra and panties. Susan flushed with embarrassment. She wondered what Brad was thinking, and how hard he was thinking it.

On Sundays, she would watch Brad at the front of the church, praying with people after the service. Once, a woman wearing something she shouldn't be wearing, let alone in church, approached Brad for prayer. Brad, a foot taller than the women, stood a few inches from her. What was he looking at? What was he thinking about? Susan fought the jealousy but finally got up and left.

What confused the whole issue more, and kept her from sorting things out, was a terrible childhood incident: a visiting evangelist had molested her as a child. She had brought this up months earlier to David and to Brad, but she still hadn't figured out how to process it. Somehow it threw a sticky web over her relationship with Brad and his addiction to pornography.

Now she couldn't untangle the mess. More and more, she needed to talk with Brad, but he had forbidden it. Susan felt increasingly trapped.

One night in late fall, they started talking about their sex lives. It had been many days since they had made love, many days since Brad had even touched her in any way. Susan asked why. Soon they were digging trenches and lobbing shells; an argument erupted.

In the middle of the fight, Brad said, "Look, I'm just going to have to try harder at being interested in you sexually. Maybe if I start journaling, I can begin to figure this out."

Susan exploded, "What? I can't believe it! You had plenty of passion for those women in the pictures! You risked everything to experience sexual fulfillment with them! But you have to journal and struggle to even touch me?"

Susan shook with an anger she didn't know was in her, but she felt she had already said too much. The fight moved on to other areas and lasted past midnight. When they started going in circles, they quit.

At that point, Susan quit. She dressed, got in her car, and drove away. She hadn't packed, but she didn't intend to return.

It seemed pitch black out; tears clouded her eyes. Soon she was crying so hard she had to pull over. "Brad, why can't you love me?" she sobbed. "What am I supposed to do!"

She began pounding the steering wheel. "Damn you women who took off your clothes! Damn you!" Waves of anger and hurt and despair swept over her. She sobbed and pounded and screamed for an hour. Finally, she muttered, "Oh God, what am I supposed to do?"

Utterly weary, she took one more step in the cold dark: she turned the car around and headed home.

December Get-Away

In late December, Brad's parents visited. Brad had arranged for them to take care of the children so he and Susan could be alone.

Brad thought it was merely a weekend away. Susan, though, had an agenda.

After her weeping explosion in the car, she knew she had to tell Brad about her anger. From August to now, she had carefully avoided telling Brad about the ugliness seething within her. Now she was going to tell him about it even if he became angry, even if it tempted him to go back to pornography. She didn't care: if he couldn't live without it, so be it. She would buy him a subscription to *Playboy*! But no longer was she going to act as if nothing was bothering her.

When they got to the retreat center where they were staying, they took a walk. Susan broached the subject: "Brad, I need to talk to you about this pornography business." Brad rolled his eyes. "Brad, you don't understand how angry I am."

"Well, then deal with it. But don't bother me!"

Susan retreated. *That's it. It's not worth it.* She stewed for a few moments. Then she thought, *No. You're at a crossroad. If you retreat now, you'll never deal with it. If you advance, maybe there's victory on the other end.*

"No. You brought it into the relationship. All those years you told me I was the problem — and I believed it. But it wasn't my problem, it was yours! Now you're going to help me work through my anger about all this. Tonight you're going to listen!"

Brad sighed, but he said nothing. Susan went on. She didn't shout, but her words were filled with plaintive passion: "Brad, don't you understand what you've done? Don't you understand what this has done to my self-esteem? All those years, I wondered why you wouldn't come to me for sex. I was more than willing. It wasn't as if I was saying don't touch me. . . ."

They talked for six hours that night, mostly Susan talking. She told him of her resentments at the risks he took, about being rejected for glossy photos, about his blaming her, about her tear-filled nights, about his stupid requests for her to wear new outfits, about their spoiled tenth anniversary, about her sexual self-doubts, about how jealous she had become, about how violated she felt.

And Brad listened.

Little Piece by Little Piece

Susan and Brad still engage in some impassioned fights, trying to sort through the residue of denial and anger. Sometimes Susan wonders if Brad will ever find fulfillment in her as he did with pornography. Sometimes she resents the time and energy the rebuilding takes. But Susan is more hopeful than ever, partly because of that talk, partly because of a dream she had a couple of weeks later.

In the dream — God-given, she believes — she and Brad stood at the front of their church's sanctuary, though not close together; they were with many other couples, all facing the seats. Suddenly a creature appeared in the center aisle. It looked like a person, but it wasn't a person; Susan knew it represented pornography.

A huge distance separated her and Brad; neither of them said anything. Susan sensed that Brad felt defeated, but she was simply frightened. Her heart pounded.

The creature started yelling and screaming, and filth came out of its mouth. Nobody did anything — a whole crowd of people, and nobody did anything. They were just watching.

Susan finally shouted at the creature, "No! You won't do that! You don't have any power in our lives anymore!" Instantly, the creature's body flew away, but his head was left sitting on the floor.

Susan thought, *There's no power left. The body's gone. I don't have to be scared any more.* They weren't moving physically, but the distance between her and Brad became less and less. Susan thought, *I don't need to be scared.*

Suddenly, though, she was frightened again: more filth started coming out of the creature's mouth. Again, she waited for someone to say something, but no one did. She realized the evil would only be defeated if God helped. So she prayed aloud, "O God, help us! Defeat this creature. Save us!"

A small piece of the head fell away and disappeared. She wondered why the whole head didn't disappear at once. So she kept praying, and the more she prayed, the more little pieces fell away and disappeared.

Finally, the head was gone. She and Brad stood together at the front of the multitude of couples. There was no more fear or sorrow; everyone was filled with hope.

Susan awoke, and she began pondering the dream. She realized that though the practice of pornography was gone, its power remained. The struggle to recapture their marriage would be a hard one. But she and Brad were not alone — other couples struggled as they did. With God's help and with fear and trembling, they had begun to reveal themselves to one another. Now they were closer than ever.

It would take a long time, long enough to make her wonder sometimes. Yet Susan was convinced that if they kept working at it, little piece by little piece, the creature would be defeated.

God has a long history of redeeming our sinful failures, of turning our worst blunders into opportunities for personal growth and spiritual development.

— Richard Exley

CHAPTER ELEVEN

After the Fall

The voice on the other end of the line was desperate. In a shaky, emotion-filled voice, the wife of a minister and mother of four confessed her adultery.

"I don't know why I'm calling you," she stammered, "except I read your book, and I thought maybe you could help me."

I began to reply, but she plowed ahead, "But I'm not sure I want help. I love Brad. He's so understanding, so caring, not like my husband who takes me for granted."

I listened for the better part of an hour while she poured out her story of a marriage undermined by the demands of ministry that won her husband's affections. She had inadvertently begun spending time with a younger man who was just a friend. Nothing more. Suddenly she was "in love." Now she was torn between her family and her lover. Her husband was growing suspicious, and her all-consuming guilt enveloped her.

Following the release of my book, *Perils of Power: Immorality in the Ministry* (Honor Books), I began receiving calls like this and visits from fallen ministers and their spouses. Although their circumstances differed, they all shared at least one thing in common — devastation.

In every case, I found myself face to face with immorality's tragic consequences. A pastor ensnared by adultery, or some other moral failure, usually loses his position, his income, and often his residence. (Since I've worked only with male ministers, I write of the experience of male pastors and their wives.) Not infrequently, he is forced to leave the very community that should be giving him emotional support. He will be asked to confess publicly and resign all hard-won places of honor.

These losses, though, are inconsequential compared to his loss of self-esteem. In telling the truth, he has destroyed his own self-image, false though it was. No longer can he pretend to be a godly man of spiritual and moral integrity. For years he has managed to live a lie, but no more. Now everyone knows, now everywhere he turns his shameful failure confronts him. His confession has destroyed the faith placed in him by his peers, his congregation, his family.

His wife and family, too, share in the consequences. Heather Bryce, a pen name of a spouse who wrote "After the Affair" in LEADERSHIP magazine, points out, "The bewildered, stunned pastor's wife suffers losses in addition to her husband's. They will move, thus costing her contact with her friends, and she may well lose her husband. At the least, she has lost her pastor. She loses her self-worth both from the adultery and from losing the ministry where she received approval. Since few people understand the whole situation, she is isolated at her point of greatest need. When able to stay within the marriage relationship, her only companion is the one who acted to her hurt."

Her past, once cherished, is tarnished. Now she is contaminated by it.

Helping such couples in crisis is draining. At times, I don't feel particularly qualified for it. Still, from time to time, I am required to play a primary role in the restoration of a pastor. Here is what I've learned as I've walked couples through their pain.

Failure or Sinful Lifestyle?

There is a difference between the minister who falls once, voluntarily confesses his sinful failure, and submits to a restoration process, and the minister trapped in an immoral lifestyle. The latter rarely confesses his sin until he is exposed — even then he may deny its full extent and resist church discipline.

Those in authority are wise to distinguish between the two. Arbitrary discipline, without regard to individual circumstances, is irresponsible. A minister should be able to confess voluntarily without fear of exposure or recrimination. If such a forum existed, in conjunction with spiritual care, many ministers could be delivered from immorality before it blossomed into a lifestyle. If the sin is not public knowledge, I see no scriptural reason why it should be publicly exposed if he has forsaken his sin, voluntarily confessed, and submitted to the proper authorities for rehabilitation.

Unfortunately, no such official forum exists. So the minister who, in a moment of weakness, gives in to temptation is trapped with the awful knowledge of his sin. The isolation he feels can make him vulnerable to further temptation. In short order, he is ensnared in immorality. What was birthed in sinful weakness has become a clandestine, immoral lifestyle. It is this situation — secret, habitual immorality — I address in this chapter.

Repeated adultery is seldom just a "sexual sin." Rather it is a complex web of issues — the way the man relates to his spouse, his self-image and sexual identity, his lifestyle and work habits. These cannot be worked through in a brief encounter or in a few days away in retreat. Nor can they be adequately addressed while the minister is still enmeshed in ministry. The pressures are simply too great, the temptation to return to the familiar routine too compelling — a routine that originally contributed to the problem. Therefore the fallen minister must be removed from active ministry if he is going to be restored both spiritually and vocationally.

Earning Trust

Pastor Ed Dobson, who played a significant role in the reha-bilitation of Truman Dollar, a well-known independent Baptist minister, says, "Restoration, to me, has two levels. The basic need is restoration to spiritual wholeness. Only after that issue is dealt with can we begin to even talk about the possibility of restoration to position."

The early sessions should focus on trust building, believes Louis McBurney, a psychiatrist who specializes in helping clergy in crisis. "It's important to bring up issues that need to be discussed," he says, "but it's especially important to build relationships."

Trust between the fallen minister and the pastor, counselor, or group must be established on several levels. First he must trust you as a person. He must be convinced you are willing and able to empathize with him — to feel and understand what he is experi-encing. Only then can he trust you.

At this juncture, he feels disenfranchised from his peers and feels his professional identity is lost. He feels more like a client than a fellow minister. To help him feel accepted as a peer, I like to meet informally, over lunch or a game of racquetball. These informal meetings are "social" and never take the place of our scheduled counseling. Although they are time consuming, an added pressure in an already over-crowded calendar, the benefits more than justify the extra effort.

I remember one emotional parting at the conclusion of a suc-cessful two-year rehabilitation. The restored minister and his wife hugged me and wept with gratitude. "I don't know what we would have done without you," the wife said. "It really made a difference the way you and your wife accepted us. The meals we shared were real life savers for me."

Her husband added, "In the office, you were 'the doctor' and I was 'the patient,' but on the racquetball court, we were just men. I was one of the guys, not just a fallen minister."

He also must have confidence in your skills. Fundamental to the whole process is his conviction of your competence, that you can help him. He must be absolutely sure his deepest secrets are safe with you, that you will always honor the sacred privilege of confidentiality.

Finally, he must know, beyond all doubt, that you are on his side, that his spiritual well-being is your highest concern. If he has the slightest doubt where your loyalties lie, the whole process will be compromised. This level of trust will not be achieved in the first session, of course — probably not in the first several sessions. Initially he may resent you, may consider you a part of the religious system that deprived him of his reputation, his ministry, and his livelihood. As the process continues, he will probably send up some trial balloons to see how you'll react.

One minister finally risked revealing to me his anger at the way his denomination handled his adultery.

"They are accusing me of being uncooperative," he spewed angrily, "simply because I'm unwilling to relocate to another city. I've tried to tell them that we own a home here, that my wife has a good job, which is our only source of income right now. But they refuse to understand. In fact, they have told me that if I don't relocate within thirty days, I will be expelled from the rehabilitation program."

He paused, waiting for my reaction. Rather than offering an opinion, I simply said, "It sounds like you feel trapped and misunderstood."

If you consistently demonstrate both compassion and competence, his trust will begin to grow.

Personal disclosures, if they are timely and appropriate, can enhance the process significantly at this point.

One minister with a long history of sexual immorality struggled with an overwhelming sense of unworthiness. He was convinced he would be doing God and the church a big favor if he dropped out of the ministry for good. He didn't believe God could forgive him. And even if God could forgive, he wasn't sure God could change him.

Nothing seemed to pierce his armor until his counselor disclosed that he too had suffered a moral failure in the early years of his ministry. Following that disclosure the fallen minister took hope. The evidence of God's grace and forgiveness was so obvious in his counselor's life that he dared to believe God could do the same for him.

One word of caution: disclose personal struggles and failures in the past tense. This accomplishes at least two things. First, it offers hope. If you've already worked through a particular temptation or difficulty, the struggling minister can point to your victory. Second, your victorious experience can lend insights for helping him with his temptations, thus reinforcing his faith. Because he knows you share that which is common to all men, he will find your counsel more credible.

The Real Issue

Once trust is established, I begin to discuss his failures. I help him process his feelings, and we try to determine the underlying issue that initially made him vulnerable to sexual temptation.

Owning sin is seldom easy, though. The truth of infidelity is terribly painful. He has grown accustomed to living with self-deceit. He has developed an elaborate system to rationalize his inexplicable behavior. In confession he experiences, maybe for the first time, the true magnitude of his sin. He suddenly sees his sin through God's eyes. He is a liar and a deceiver. His immorality has made a mockery out of his faith, his marriage, and his ministry. In the agony of that moment, he will be tempted to withhold some of the details. He will probably attempt to justify his actions.

Take Bill, for example. He avoided detection for more than fourteen years, having been involved in a series of affairs. Even after being confronted with his immorality, he resisted confessing the magnitude of his sin. His wife writes, "It took six days of confrontation to extract all the facts. Through clever hedging and conscious lying, Bill had covered the extent of his immoral actions."

While understandable, refusing to come fully clean only

delays the healing process. And painful though it may be, the counselor must hold the man's feet to the fire; he must come clean. But often the man doesn't have the stomach for it; the pain is more than he can admit even to himself. Over a few days, perhaps two to three weeks, he will finally tell all. The results are traumatic — for him and his wife — wide swings of emotion ranging from almost uncontrollable rage to numbing grief.

The help of a pastor, counselor, or support group is invaluable during this period.

In *Beyond Forgiveness*, Don Baker tells of the discipline and restoration of a staff minister named Greg. Baker confesses, "One of the many mistakes I made during Greg's twenty-six month restoration period was that I failed to maintain constant contact with him. In fact, Greg admitted later that he felt that I and other members of the staff had let him down. One staff person took him to lunch — once. I met with him occasionally and called periodically, but we never established a routine."

They had been Greg's closest friends, the ones to whom he looked for support. But during his ordeal, he had almost no fellowship with them. They were gracious when they ran into him, but they never went out of their way to connect with him or his wife.

Greg was invited to join a group of five men who met weekly for breakfast and spiritual fellowship.

"They accepted him completely," Baker writes. "They treated him as a human being and as an equal. There was no condemnation, no criticism. No conditions were imposed upon their continuing relationship. They had breakfast together, shared needs with each other, and prayed." They became a major force in his recovery.

Cracking the Lifestyle

Ministers who fall prey to sexual temptation are often driven people, workaholics whose lifestyle cause their most important relationships to suffer. Helping them regain control is critical. They must learn new ways of dealing with the pressures of life.

One minister I counseled was obviously a type-A personality, but the drivenness contributing to his moral failure remained unchecked. His old way of dealing with stress was to immerse himself in ministry (now in his new line of work), isolating himself from his wife and family. Of course, this only amplified his stress. This cycle fed itself, leaving him stressed out and susceptible to sexual temptation.

With his wife, I explored with him the source of his driven-ness. At its root was a lack of self-esteem. No amount of success could enable him to escape his self-doubt. In fact the more success-ful he became, the harder he pushed himself. He was convinced that if other people really knew him the way he knew himself, they would know what a phony he really was.

Using both Scripture and reason, I helped him see there was not enough success in the world to still the tormenting voices within. Over time he came to appreciate his value as a person simply because of who he was — a man created in the image of God — not because of any success he might achieve. The Scrip-tures, rather than his emotions, became the foundation for his self-worth. He learned to share his fears with his wife, and in prayer they combated the inner enemies that sought to destroy him. Little by little, his drivenness was replaced by self-acceptance.

Attention should also be given to spiritual disciplines. Often a fallen pastor's devotional life centers around power rather than intimacy; he's looking for strength to succeed rather than an experi-ence of God's love. He has only a "working relationship" with God. His reading, if he takes time to read at all, is generally in the area of church growth and professional development.

So I require him to read for spiritual enrichment, to focus on his own spiritual needs. Required reading includes *My Utmost For His Highest* by Oswald Chambers, *A Testament of Devotion* by Thomas R. Kelly, *Celebration of Discipline* by Richard Foster, and *Ordering Your Private World* by Gordon MacDonald, as well as my books, *Perils of Power* and *The Rhythm of Life*.

Probing Marital Wounds

Critical to the restoration process is the minister's relationship with his wife. Most of the wives I've counseled were determined to stand by their husbands. But the healing of their marriage was, nonetheless, a lengthy and difficult process.

Her emotions swing. She has discovered that her husband isn't the man she married. That man was good and godly, incapable of the kind of things this man has done — unspeakable things, sinful things beyond her comprehension. Not only has he done them, but he has confessed them to her in sordid detail. She had trusted him. She never thought to question his late hours. She believed him when he told her his preoccupation was church-related. But now her trust is gone, crushed beneath the awful revelation of his unfaithfulness.

Yet she wants to save their marriage. She badly wants to forgive him as much as he wants to be forgiven. Can she? Can she get rid of her hurt and anger without destroying him — and their relationship? Can she learn to trust him again, respect him as a godly man, as the spiritual leader in their home? These and a hundred more questions haunt her.

Before her wound can heal, though, she must work through her feelings. During this process, the presence of a compassionate Christian counselor is mandatory. The counselor serves as both a nonjudgmental listener and a spiritual facilitator. The counselor holds her accountable, helps her deal with the hurts and anger she might otherwise gloss over or bury. Anger and bitterness must be acknowledged and confessed before forgiveness can truly be extended to the offending spouse.

To survive her husband's repeated adulteries, Jeanne (not her real name) created an elaborate denial system. She simply refused to admit to herself that he might be unfaithful. Once his moral failures were made public, that same web of denial made it nearly impossible for her to feel the deep emotions of betrayal. She denied her hurt and anger, hid her feelings beneath a "Christian" facade, but on the inside she was raging.

In desperation, I suggested she write a letter to God, telling him exactly what Larry had done and how it made her feel.

"Don't edit your feelings," I counseled her. "God won't be shocked. He knows you better than you know yourself."

She tried to assure me she had already forgiven Larry, that there was nothing to tell. Gently I insisted, and reluctantly she agreed to give it a try.

When she arrived for her next session, she was barely seated before she extracted a manuscript-size letter from her purse. I commented on it.

"Once I got started," she said, holding it up, "I couldn't seem to stop. It all came rushing back — all the lies, the sneaking around, the deceit. And the anger — boy, did I get angry! I felt things I didn't know I was capable of feeling. If Larry had been there I might have tried to hurt him." Seeing this quiet woman rage was something to behold. Years of stubbornly denied hurt and anger gave her words an awful intensity.

"For the first time in my life," she continued, "I realized how much I hate him. He's destroyed my life, our children, our family — everything. I've always been the model wife and mother, and what do I get for all my efforts? A husband who sleeps with my best friend!"

"And her!" she snarled, contempt making her voice thick. "How could she pretend to be my friend? How could she look me in the eye knowing she had been with my husband? She still wants to be friends. Can you believe that?"

During this process, Jeanne faced two dangers. Initially she was tempted to deny her feelings, to avoid the whole painful process. She wanted to hurry on to forgiveness, to put the entire sordid episode behind her. By insisting she write the letter, I helped her overcome that temptation, only to be confronted by a new danger: Once she started to feel deeply, she wanted to indulge her emotions. She felt justified in her anger and wanted to punish Larry, wanted to make him suffer the way she had suffered.

I encouraged her, as I have others, to deal properly with her anger: "Jeanne, there are basically three ways of dealing with anger. The first is the world's way — express it. Take your revenge, get even. That way has a certain appeal, especially when you've been hurt. But it is terribly destructive. The second way is often the church's way — repress it. Most Christians shove it down, bury it deep inside themselves. That's what you did for years. I don't have to tell you how debilitating that can be.

"The third way is God's way — confess it. Tell God exactly how you feel. Pour your hurt and anger out to him. That's what you did when you wrote the letter. But you can't get stuck there. You've got to release your anger, let go of it. If you don't, confession does nothing but recycle your anger."

I reminded her that forgiveness is an act of the will. We begin by telling God how we really feel, that we don't want to forgive, but that, in obedience to his Word, we choose to do it anyway. Then we give God permission to change our feelings, to replace our hurt and anger with new love. Then we must forgive specifically each sin the person has committed against us.

When she asked for more guidance, I suggested a prayer. I added that since she had not been sinned against generally but specifically, she needed to forgive the sinful act specifically.

She nodded, and in a voice I had to strain to hear, she prayed, "God, you know that the very thought of the things Larry did with that woman makes me sick. When I look at him, I keep imagining them together. Sometimes I just want to run away, so I never have to see him again, but I can't. I don't want to forgive him. I want to get even, I want to hurt him, but I know that's not right. Please, God, help me to forgive him."

She took a deep breath. "God, I choose to forgive Larry for having sex with Rachel. I choose to forgive him for betraying me and the covenant of marriage."

Jeanne prayed for a long time that afternoon, dealing with one painful incident after another. When she finished, I asked her if she would like to destroy the letter she had written to God.

"It's a symbol of your feelings, of all the things you've held against Larry," I said. "When you tear it up and drop it in the wastebasket, you are releasing your feelings, letting go of your hurt and anger."

With trembling hands, she slowly shredded the letter and let the fragments fall from her fingers into the wastebasket. When she finished, tears were running down her cheeks. She said, "I feel different. I really do."

Rebuilding the Broken World

Before the cycle of forgiveness was complete, Jeanne had to confront Larry with the truth of what his adulteries had done to her. During this time, more than once Larry pleaded, "Must you tell me all of this? Can't we let bygones be bygones?"

Jeanne might have yielded to his pleadings had she not been convinced that Larry's only hope was coming to grips with the full extent of his sin. He could fully repent only if he saw his sin through her eyes, only if he fully felt everything she had suffered. As the apostle Paul writes in 2 Corinthians 7:10, "Godly sorrow brings repentance that leads to salvation and leaves no regret."

Confronting Larry was different from confessing her feelings to God. Then she was pouring herself before God. But the object of her wrath was not present, so no one got hurt. This time she told Larry the effects of his behavior. Her purpose was not to wound him but to confront him with the tragic consequences of his sin.

This phase was painfully slow and fraught with crises — like the time Larry had car trouble and was late getting home but didn't bother to call. When he finally walked through the door, Jeanne was raging.

"Where have you been?" she demanded. Without giving him a chance to reply, she continued, "Who is it this time?"

When he tried to explain, she cut him off. He then cut her off: "I'm not going to live like this the rest of my life. If you are going to throw the past up to me every time I'm a few minutes late, there's no hope for us!"

They argued for a long time that night. They finally called me and asked me to come over. I sat in their small living room and worked to help them understand what was happening: "Larry, your adulteries have destroyed Jeanne's trust. In the past you were often late, and she thought nothing about it. Now she knows you were lying to her, that you made a fool out of her. She's not going to let that happen again."

"But I've told her I will never be unfaithful again," Larry protested. He turned to Jeanne. "Don't you believe me?"

"I want to, Larry," Jeanne said, "but it's going to take some time."

I then read to them from Richard Dobbins's book *Saints in Crises:* "When an adulterous relationship has broken that bridge of trust, then building it back again frequently requires a healing period ranging from six months to two years . . . [the adulterous spouse] must realize that his infidelity has given his mate just cause to be both jealous and suspicious. . . . The mate who breaks the trust should volunteer information required for the mate whose trust has been shaken to check up on his whereabouts. Discovering that he is in the place he is supposed to be, doing what he said he would be doing, will help to rebuild that trust."

Chasing Little Foxes

Although adultery is the most obvious problem in the fallen minister's marriage, it is certainly not the only one. Larry and Jeanne's marriage did not suddenly fail; adultery was not the problem as much as the consequence, the culmination of several small things that went undetected. They had to give these "little foxes" their undivided attention. They had to be rectified to prevent their marriage from mediocrity and another episode of adultery.

For Don and Sherry (not their real names), the issue was busyness. With a first grader and two preschoolers, Sherry had her hands full. By the end of the day, she was exhausted. She loved her husband, but running the house and taking care of the children took all of her energy. For his part, Don was always busy with the church and never seemed to have time to help her. She tried to understand, but she resented the long hours he put in. She began to complain.

This only added to Don's frustrations, which were already stretched as a result of a strained relationship with the church board. Desperately he threw himself into ministry. He was convinced that when the board saw how hard he worked, the long hours he put in, they would appreciate him more. His long hours only served to distance him further from Sherry and the children. Eventually the pressure and loneliness became so great, he became involved with another woman.

Following Don's affair, Don and Sherry came to me for counseling. By this time, busyness had become for them a way of life. Besides working through the adultery, they had to reorder their priorities. Don made a commitment to protect his day off at all costs and to spend it with his family. He also determined to become more involved around the house and with the children. Sherry made a conscious effort to give Don the special attention he wanted.

And when these "little foxes" are attended to, the relationship is not only healed but can end up being better than the old marriage.

Evaluating Progress

One of the weightier responsibilities the pastor or committee has is evaluating the progress of the person they are restoring. Often their input determines when, and under what conditions, the pastor may return to active ministry. Therefore developing objective guidelines for measuring progress is critical.

Every minister I have worked with was initially angry — angry at his former congregation for the way it handled the situation, angry with his denominational officials for what he perceived to be insensitive and arbitrary decisions, angry with those involved in the restoration process. Rather than addressing his own failures, he insists on finding fault with the process. When a man stops being angry and blaming others, I take note of it. It is a sure sign of progress.

Bishop William Frey, president of Trinity Episcopal School for Ministry in Ambridge, Pennsylvania, looks for how much control the fallen minister tries to exercise over his own therapy: "Is he self-diagnosing and self-prescribing, or is he willing to trust the therapist or the group? I don't trust somebody who says, 'Here's my disease, and here's the treatment that you ought to give me.' "

Another sign of progress is the way the pastor sees himself. Initially, he has limited self-knowledge and tends to talk about his accomplishments — achievements around which his self-image is centered. As he makes progress toward wholeness, he will develop a greater self-understanding. This will be reflected in the way he talks about himself. His comments should begin to focus on who he is rather than what he has done — on being rather than doing.

Pastor Edward Dobson reports that Truman Dollar learned that his significance and value to God was not determined by whether or not he was in ministry or by the size of his church.

"He also learned more clearly," writes Dobson, "the importance of a personal relationship with God, not just a professional relationship with God. He learned balance. He's now convinced that it's okay to take time off to relax, to exercise, to spend time with his family — to be something besides a pastor of a big church."

Lifestyle changes also mark progress. Before his moral failure was uncovered, the fallen minister was probably over-investing in ministry at the expense of his marriage and family. That's not something he can change overnight, but it is mandatory he gets control of his schedule. When I see evidence of a balance between work and rest, worship and play, I know he is making progress.

"Another way to assess a person's progress," says Louis McBurney, "is to get feedback from the spouse. . . . The man may be able to put the mask on or say the right things in public, but the spouse is going to tell us, 'Well, I'm still worried about him,' and she will identify unresolved issues."

Sometimes it is not just what she says, but her body language. I've seen a wife cross her legs, fold her arms, and bend forward when her husband was saying something she knew, and I later discovered, wasn't true. By the same token, when she genuinely affirms her husband's progress, you can usually be assured real progress is being made.

Back into It

Once emotional and spiritual wholeness has been restored, we can turn our attention toward restoration to ministry. This process should include at least three stages: (1) supervised ministry in the local church, (2) selected preaching engagements, and (3) full and unrestricted ministry as the Lord directs.

This will resurrect a host of conflicting emotions. He is excited yet also filled with dread. *Am I really ready? Can I handle the unique pressures and stress of ministry? How will a return to ministry effect my wife and family?* The supervised stage of restoration will give him and his family an opportunity to work through their initial concerns without the constant demands of their own congregation.

The minister often finds himself in a dilemma regarding his past moral failure. Unless he was highly visible, most congregations who may consider calling him will be unaware of his fall. How much should he tell them, and when? If he discloses everything up front, will they even consider him?

I believe a full disclosure during the interview with the pulpit committee is mandatory. Deception is at the heart of adultery, and a decision to keep this information from the pulpit committee may open the door for a return to a life of half-truths and self-deception.

Of equal concern to me is the minister's state of mind. If he doesn't tell them of his moral failure, he will always live in fear they will find out. No one should live under that kind of pressure. And should the pulpit committee discover his moral failure later, they will feel betrayed and doubt his integrity. As difficult as it may be, a full disclosure of the facts, though not the details, seems best.

Moral failure does not have to end as a disaster. God has a long history of redeeming our sinful failures, of turning our worst blunders into opportunities for personal growth and spiritual development. If a minister's fall is a time for great grief, then his restoration should be a time for a sacred celebration.

The final official act in the restoration process should be a public service in which the minister is officially restored to ministry. Such a service provides closure for the minister and his family, and those involved in his restoration. It publicly confirms his successful restoration and announces to the church he is once again fit for ministry.

Few experiences in life can match the holy splendor of that moment.

Part 3
The Long View

The great Christians have had great besetting sins.
— Mark Galli

CHAPTER TWELVE

When Sin
Won't Let Go

He had been preaching in his church for years, but the longer he preached, the more discouraged he grew. People just didn't get it. They gladly heard him, but instead of rising to discipleship, they slithered into lethargy. Everyone praised his preaching, but he complained, "No one acts accordingly, but instead the people become so crude, cold, and lazy that it is a shame."

For instance, he started teaching that worship is primarily an act of gratitude to God. Attending worship, he said, did not earn points with God. People loved the new teaching. And worship attendance dropped.

At one point, he was so fed up, he announced he would no longer preach to his congregation; he went on strike.

The "necessity of preaching" couldn't keep him away from the pulpit for long, but anger and resentment dogged him his whole life. A year before he died, while on a trip, he decided not to return to his home town or church. He wrote his wife, "My heart has become cold, so that I do not like to be there any longer." People were indifferent to his preaching. Some had begun to mock him, asking him what gave him the right to question everything they had been taught.

"I am tired of this city and do not wish to return," he wrote. He would rather "eat the bread of a beggar than torture and upset my poor old age and final days with the filth at Wittenberg."

It took the determined efforts of city elders to convince Martin Luther to return.

This is not the Martin Luther we've grown to know and love. That Martin Luther boldly faced the ecclesiastical machinery of medieval Catholicism, not to mention the military might of the Holy Roman Empire, declaring, "Here I stand, and I can do no other!" That Martin Luther was a decisive and penetrating theologian who recovered the grand essentials: Scripture only, faith only, grace only.

But this Martin Luther? Saints aren't supposed to be angry. Christian heroes aren't supposed to give up.

And pastors aren't supposed to sin as much as we do. In our honest moments, we admit that we are not the leaders others have come to know and love. They hear us proclaim righteousness on Sunday morning, but they don't see us at the drug store when we peek at *Penthouse*. They know we counsel with empathy and compassion, but they haven't heard us rage at our spouses in fits of temper.

As pastors, teachers, and Christian leaders, we each have a besetting sin: lust, greed, temper, sloth, whatever. We struggle to overcome it, praying, pleading, fasting, straining. But it doesn't go away. It may get worse.

We begin to wonder what in the world we're doing in ministry. "How can God use someone like me? How can I, with this persistent sin, make any contribution to the kingdom?"

As a pastor with my share of besetting sins, I thought long and hard and often about such questions. I found answers only when I began studying the lives of former preachers, people like Martin Luther and George Whitefield, great Christians with great besetting sins.

Angry Teacher of Grace

Luther, by his own account, was an angry man, though he chalked it up to providence: "I was born to war with fanatics and devils. Thus my books are very stormy and bellicose. I must root out the stumps and trunks, hew away the thorns and briar, fill in the puddles. I am a rough woodsman, who must pioneer and hew a path."

We're not surprised, then, by his views of Roman Catholicism: "We should take him — the pope, the cardinals, and whatever riffraff belongs to His Idolatrous and Papal Holiness — and (as blasphemers) tear out their tongues from the back, and nail them on the gallows."

For this anger, we have some sympathy. Luther was grappling with a corrupt and entrenched church bureaucracy, and sometimes righteous anger seemed the only leverage: "I cannot deny that I am more vehement than I should be. . . . But they assail me with God's Word so atrociously and criminally that . . . these monsters are carrying me beyond the bounds of moderation."

Often, though, Luther's anger was anything but providential or righteous. Take his attitude toward the poor.

In 1524, weary of oppression and enthused by Luther's reforms, German peasants revolted against their lords. To help bring peace, Luther wrote, *An Admonition to Peace*, in which he blamed the unrest on the rulers, saying many of the demands of the peasants were just. He also warned the peasants that the gospel taught obedience to secular rulers and the humble suffering of injustice.

The treatise calmed little, and the peasant unrest spread.

Luther was enraged, and he dashed off *Against the Robbing and Murdering Horde of Peasants*. In it he not-so-compassionately exhorted rulers to "smite, strangle, and stab [the peasants], secretly or openly, for nothing can be more poisonous, hurtful, devilish than a rebel. It is just as when one must kill a mad dog; if you do not strike him, he will strike you and a whole land with you!"

Or take Luther's attitude toward Jews.

In 1543, he wrote one of his most disturbing tracts: *On the Jews and Their Lies*. Luther was deeply disturbed by Jewish unbelief. His pastoral solution? "Set fire to their synagogues or schools." Jewish houses should be razed, and Jewish prayer books and Talmudic writings, "in which such idolatry, lies, cursing, and blasphemy are taught," should be confiscated. In addition, their rabbis should be "forbidden to teach on pain of loss of life and limb."

He urged that "safe conduct on the highways be abolished completely for the Jews," and that "all cash and treasure of silver and gold be taken from them." Though earlier he had criticized Catholics for treating Jews as dogs, toward the end of his life he said, "We are at fault for not slaying them!"

Finally, take Luther's attitude toward his allies, his fellow reformers.

In the late 1520s, he got into a running argument about the Lord's Supper with reformer Ulrich Zwingli. Zwingli believed that the bread and wine were merely symbolic of Christ's presence at the table. Luther believed Christ was present "in, with, and under" the elements.

When a pamphlet war threatened to fragment the reformation movement, Prince Philip of Hesse became concerned. He wanted Protestants to present a united front against Catholics, especially if military action was initiated by Charles V, the Holy Roman Emperor. So Philip sponsored a Protestant summit at Marburg in October 1529. He invited the leading reformers of Germany and Switzerland: Luther and his colleague Phillip Melanchthon, Ulrich Zwingli, Martin Bucer, and John Oecolampadius.

The participants quickly reached agreement on fourteen of fifteen theological points. But on the fifteenth, on the presence of

Christ in the sacraments, the conference floundered.

When Zwingli put forth his symbolic interpretation, Luther quoted from the Latin Bible: "Hoc est corpus meum!" (This is my body). He took a piece of chalk and scribbled the words on the table.

John Oecolampadius offered a counter-text: "The Spirit gives life; the flesh counts for nothing" (John 6:63). Luther was unmoved: "Again and again the body of Christ is eaten, for he himself commands us so. If he ordered me to eat dung, I would do it, since I would altogether know that it would be to my salvation!"

Luther felt Zwingli acted "like an ass," quoting biblical Greek whenever he had a chance. Zwingli, for his part, felt Luther was condescending. Soon, discussions broke off. Later in the day, Luther snapped to Martin Bucer, who leaned toward Zwingli's theology, "It is evident that we do not have the same spirit!"

Eventually, a carefully worded compromise was reached (the sacrament was a divine gift of grace with a "spiritual benefit"). But within weeks, a split in the reformation ranks reopened. Luther summed up his feelings: "One side in this controversy belongs to the Devil and is God's enemy." He didn't mean his side.

Thirteen years later, Luther continued to grumble about the conference: "I've bitten into many a nut, believing it was good, only to find it wormy. Zwingli and Erasmus are nothing but wormy nuts that taste like crap in one's mouth!"

Though all of the reformers at Marburg share responsibility for the rupture, it's clear that Luther was much less conciliatory than the others. This had disastrous consequences for the church. One historian notes that this "set a pattern for Protestant non-cooperation that has lasted to today. . . . All genuine followers of Jesus Christ will sorrow for the chance for Protestant unity that was lost in the sixteenth century."

In short, Luther's besetting sin was anger. He was in many respects a violent, coarse, ill-tempered, cranky man. He was also used mightily by God to recover, oddly enough, the doctrine of grace.

Through faith by grace — this theme permeates his commentaries, which both Protestants and Catholics today draw on for insight. Take a passage from his commentary on Galatians:

"Christ, according to the proper and true definition, is no Moses, no lawgiver, no tyrant, but a mediator for sins, a free giver of grace, righteousness, and life; who gave himself, not for our merits, holiness, righteousness, and godly life, but for our sins."

Grace saturates his catechisms, even where we don't expect it. For instance, in his *Small Catechism*, he expounds on the first article of the Apostle's Creed ("I believe in God, the Father Almighty, Maker of heaven and earth"):

"I believe that God has created me and all that exists; that he has given and still preserves to me my body and soul, my eyes and ears, and all members, my reasons and all the power of my soul, together with food and raiment, home and family, and all my property; that he daily provides abundantly for all the needs of my life, protects me from all danger, and guards and keeps me from all evil; and that he does this purely out of fatherly and divine goodness and mercy, without merit in me."

Grace accents his hymns, sung throughout Christendom today, especially his masterpiece, *A Mighty Fortress Is Our God:*

> Did we in our own strength confide,
> Our striving would be losing;
> Were not the right man on our side,
> The man of God's own choosing.
> Dost ask who that may be?
> Christ Jesus it is He,
> Lord Sabaoth His name,
> From age to age the same,
> And He must win the battle.

Through faith by grace: the great contribution of Martin Luther, the angry man.

Cold Evangelist of God's Love

George Whitefield could preach. The skeptical Benjamin Franklin noted, "Every accent, every emphasis, every modulation of the voice, was so perfectly well turned and well placed, that, without being interested in the subject, one could not help being pleased with the discourse."

Franklin should know. In his *Autobiography*, the frugal printer wrote, "I happened . . . to attend one of his [Whitefield's] sermons, in the course of which I perceived he intended to finish with a collection, and I silently resolved he should get nothing from me."

The collection was for Whitefield's Georgia orphanage, which Franklin thought ill-planned, and he had told Whitefield so. Thus for some time, he had refused to give to it.

At this sermon, though, Franklin says, "I had in my pocket a handful of copper money, three or four silver dollars, and five pistoles in gold. As he proceeded I began to soften, and concluded to give the coppers. Another stroke of his oratory made me ashamed of that, and determined me to give the silver; and he finished so admirably that I emptied my pocket wholly into the collector's dish, gold and all."

Whitefield had amazing gifts of oratory, and he used those gifts mostly to tell millions — and tell them passionately and convincingly — of the warm, loving gift of God's love.

On the other hand, he was a mess when it came to personal relationships, especially with women.

When the 25-year-old Whitefield met young Elizabeth Delamotte in England, he found himself falling in love. That bothered him. His passion for her, he felt, might steal the passion he felt for Christ. He became so troubled that, as he set sail for America in 1739, he decided simply to put her out of his mind.

When he arrived in Georgia, though, a letter awaited him. It was from Delamotte. He read it and became anxious again. He wrote her back, trying to keep a safe emotional distance: "What room can there be for God, when a rival hath taken possession of the heart?" Still, he had to admit he was attracted to her: "I could almost drop a tear, and wish myself, for a moment or two, in England. But hush, nature."

In the next few weeks, Whitefield's *Journals* report "unspeakable troubles and anguish of soul," presumably as he debated whether he should ask for Delamotte's hand. Finally, he concluded he should.

But even after that decision, he couldn't bring himself to express simply and forthrightly his love for Delamotte. His proposal letters sound more like business transactions.

To her parents, he wrote, "I find by experience, that a mistress is absolutely necessary for the due management of my increasing family [orphanage]. . . . It hath been therefore much impressed upon my heart that I should marry, in order to have a help meet for me in the work whereunto our dear Lord Jesus hath called me."

When he wrote to Delamotte, he began by cataloguing the sufferings she would endure as his wife. He concluded with the less-than-endearing, "Can you, when you have a husband, be as though you had none, and willingly part with him, even for a long season, when his Lord and Master shall call him forth to preach the Gospel?"

And lest she be confused about his intentions, he made clear the role of romance in his offer: "I write not from any other principles but the love of God. . . . The passionate expressions which carnal courtiers use . . . ought to be avoided by those that would marry in the Lord."

As one historian put it, "Had he tried to design his proposal in such a way as to ensure its failure, he could hardly have done better."

In fact, Delamotte turned him down.

Still, Whitefield believed he was called to marriage, and when he mentioned this to fellow evangelist Howell Harris, Harris discerned "an amazingly providential solution."

Harris had fallen in love with one Elizabeth James, a Welsh widow in her mid-thirties. Though her affection for him was equally strong, he, like Whitefield, wanted "no creature between my soul and God." He had labored to break off the relationship but failed.

Harris arranged a meeting between Whitefield and James. Whitefield was impressed with her devotion to Christ, so both Harris and Whitefield wrote her, suggesting an exchange of suitors.

James was furious, writing Harris, "If you were my own father you had no right of disposing me against my will." Still, she didn't close the door to Whitefield, and as they corresponded over the next months, Whitefield became convinced the match was right. James "objected much," Harris reported, because of "her regards to me and that she could not help it still."

Yet, four days later, she agreed to marry Whitefield. At the wedding a few weeks hence, Whitefield allowed Howell Harris to give away the bride.

Whitefield had earlier vowed he "would not preach one sermon less in a married than in a single state," and now he seemed intent on keeping the vow. During the week-long honeymoon in James' home, he preached twice a day. That set a precedent: for the rest of his career Whitefield itinerated, for the most part leaving James to fend for herself in their London home.

In spite of feeling called to marriage, Whitefield found this most intimate of relationships an annoyance. Within two months of his wedding, he wrote, "Oh, for that blessed time when we shall neither marry nor be given in marriage, but be as the angels of God." Certainly, when James died, he mourned her passing, but late in the marriage he still warned a young man, "Marry when or whom you will, expect trouble in the flesh."

As for James, she was never emotionally satisfied with Whitefield. Her letters show it took her ten years to get over Harris. She suffered three miscarriages, and her only child with Whitefield, a son, died when four months old.

A man who lived with the couple during their last years said more than he intended when he wrote, "He did not intentionally make his wife unhappy. He always preserved great decency and decorum in his conduct towards her."

Which was exactly the problem. Whitefield was a cold, aloof, awkward lover.

So guess how God used him: to spread with warmth and passion the intimate love of God. His preaching, in contrast to his love letters, brimmed with emotion:

"My friends," he concludes one sermon, "I would preach with all my heart till midnight, to do you good, till I could preach no more. Oh, that this body might hold out to speak more for my dear

Redeemer! Had I a thousand lives, had I a thousand tongues, they should be employed in inviting sinners to come to Jesus Christ!

"Come, then, let me prevail with some of you to come along with me. Come, poor, lost, undone sinner, come just as you are to Christ, and say, 'If I be damned, I will perish at the feet of Jesus Christ, where never one perished yet.' He will receive you with open arms; the dear Redeemer is willing to receive you all."

This passion, unusual for that day, helped spark revivals in England and Scotland, and the Great Awakening in America. When Whitefield passed through communities, people were electrified. In October 1740, for instance, Nathan Cole, a Connecticut farmer, heard from a neighbor that Whitefield was scheduled to preach nearby. He later recorded his reaction:

"I was in my field at work; I had dropped my tool that I had in my hand and ran home to my wife, telling her to make ready quickly to go hear Mr. Whitefield preach at Middletown, then run to my pasture for my horse with all my might, fearing that I should be too late."

As he made his way to Middletown, about twelve miles away, he saw hundreds of horses: "Every horse seemed to go with all his might to carry his rider to hear news from heaven for saving of souls." He noted "ferry boats [on the Connecticut River] running swift backward and forward, bringing over loads of people." Furthermore, "The land and banks over the river looked black with people and horses. All along the 12 miles I saw no man at work in his field, but all seemed to have gone."

When Whitefield preached, he said, "He looked as if he was clothed with authority from the Great God, and a sweet solemn solemnity sat upon his brow, and my hearing him preach gave me a heart wound. By God's blessing my old foundation was broken up, and I saw that my righteousness would not save me."

This story was repeated thousands of times in Whitefield's long evangelistic career. People adored his preaching and were enraptured with his every word. Through the preaching of an aloof lover, thousands came to know the tender, intimate love of God.

A Power Greater than Sin

The French mystic François Fénelon said, "I have found that God leaves, even in the most spiritual people, certain weaknesses which seem to be entirely out of place." And the history of the church and the Bible are replete with examples. Time and again, God leaves in individuals a sin entirely out of place:

The cowardly Moses successfully leads a revolt from the greatest military power of the day.

The jellyfish Peter becomes the rock of the church.

The ambitious, adulterous, murderous David becomes the author of many Psalms, the most sublime of religious poetry.

It makes you wonder about your own besetting sin, or sins. Paul wrote, "I beat my body and make it my slave so that after I have preached to others, I myself will not be disqualified for the prize" (1 Cor. 9:27). And so, naturally, we will continue to struggle against the flesh.

But Luther and Whitefield, among many others, show us that we no longer need ask, "Can God use me, with this besetting sin? For a pastor, isn't this so entirely out of place?"

Of course, and of course.

While temptation is inevitable, it's not irresistible.
— *David Goetz*

Epilogue

Deception is the art of flyfishing.

The experienced flyfisherman ties — not buys — his flies. He intimately knows which bugs trout are feeding on in any given season. On the spot, he builds an imitation to match what the fish are feeding on — a Mayfly, a mosquito, a caddis fly. He takes a naked hook half the length of a stick pin and attaches a bouquet of hackle, thread, and color.

Then the next deception: casting an imitation bug and (without cursing) delicately, convincingly presenting it to the wily trout.

For the Evil One, deception is also an art. Sin is often camouflaged as the good — that's what makes the temptations of ministry so hard to detect. They're often cast alongside the genuine article: Naked ambition next to a godly zeal. Romantic attraction beside pastoral concern. Bitterness alongside righteous anger.

While temptation is inevitable, it's not irresistible. In the previous pages, the authors have shown us some of the evil that is disguised as good. They've told us we don't have to bite on every temptation that comes our way. And they've reminded us of the great promise: "No temptation has seized you except what is common to man. And God is faithful; he will not let you be tempted beyond what you can bear. But when you are tempted, he will also provide a way out so that you can stand up under it" (1 Cor. 10:13).

Our prayer is that this book has helped you better discern deception and so provide a way out.